THE

PRINCIPLES

OF

LOGIC,

FOR

HIGH SCHOOLS AND COLLEGES.

BY

A. SCHUYLER, M. A.,

PROFESSOR OF MATHEMATICS AND LOGIC IN BALDWIN UNIVERSITY

VAN ANTWERP, BRAGG & CO.,

137 WALNUT STREET, CINCINNATI. 28 BOND STREET, NEW YORK.

ELECTROTYPED AT
FRANKLIN TYPE FOUNDRY,
CINCINNATI.

ECLECTIC PRESS:
VAN ANTWERP, BRAGG & CO.,
CINCINNATI.

PREFACE.

THE author has endeavored, in the following treatise, to give a clear, concise, and systematic development of the principles of Logic.

Care has been taken to retain the valuable results of the labors of former investigators—results which the world can not afford to lose; yet much will be found that is new, not only in the methods, but also in the matter.

The works of the following authors have been examined: Aristotle, Hamilton, Mill, De Morgan, Thompson, Mansel, Whately, Wilson, Tappan, Mahan, Day, McGregor, True, and Coppée. To Hamilton, the author is especially indebted for valuable aid in reference to the following subjects: Classification of Science, General Outline, Concepts, and Modified Logic; and to Mill, for examples illustrating the four experimental methods of investigation.

It has been kept steadily in mind that the work is designed for a text-book; and, in accordance with this design, a topical arrangement has been given to the matter, so as to adapt it to the topical method of conducting recitations, which, when followed up by appropriate questions, is, of all methods, the best for the grade of students who will pursue the study of Logic.

It will add much to the interest and value of the recitation, to require the student to write out upon the blackboard, the classifications and all other matter whose condensed form renders it practicable.

This practice will induce thorough preparation and secure the advantages resulting from the prevalent excellent methods of conducting mathematical recitations.

Euler's notation, which has been extensively employed, will be found to add greatly to clearness in apprehending the principles. This practice has been censured by Mansel on the ground that "a concept can not be presented to the senses." To this it may be replied that this notation is designed to represent, not the concepts themselves, which it can not adequately do, but the *relation* of the concepts, and this it accurately accomplishes.

Intuitions have been treated summarily, not in detail, and under this head are included not only the ultimate facts of reason, but also the ultimate facts of external perception, called by Kant *Sense-intuitions*, and the ultimate facts of consciousness.

We invite special attention to the following topics: The Fundamental Laws of Thought, Opposition, Conversion, Principles warranting (A), (E), (I), (O), Determination of the Valid Moods, Discussion of the Figures, Positive Propositions and Syllogisms, Induction and Fallacies.

Some Logicians have discarded the Fourth Figure, on the ground that there can be but three, to wit: The middle term may be the subject of one premise and the predicate of the other, the predicate of both premises, or the subject of both. But in the first case there are two varieties: the middle term may be the subject of the major premise and predicate of the minor, or it may be the predicate of the major and subject of the minor.

In this connection, it is important to observe that the major term is simply the predicate of the conclusion, and not necessarily greater than the minor term, and that the major premise is the premise containing the major term. If the Fourth Figure could not be justified on its own grounds, there are historical reasons for retaining it.

Though the laws of validity warranting the conclusions (A), (E), (I), (O) have been exhibited (pp. 48–50), irrespective of the doctrine of Figure and Mood, yet no scholar can afford to remain in ignorance of these subjects which display so high a degree of ingenuity and so many points of interest.

The reduction, direct and indirect, of the other figures to the first will be found to be not so laborious and disgusting a process as has sometimes been represented, but, if thoroughly done, will prove a most interesting and profitable exercise, since it will render the student familiar with the Figures, Moods, and Names of the various syllogisms, as well as show that all can be brought to the test of Aristotle's Dictum.

In Mathematical Induction, general propositions are rigorously demonstrated, the premises of the demonstration being a particular case ascertained by trial, and the demonstrated principle, that if any case is true, the next is true. Then, by going back to the case ascertained by trial, we have the warrant for concluding that since that case is true, the next is true, and the next, and so on; that is, that the general proposition including all these particular cases is true.

Mathematical science then, has not for its exclusive basis, a few fundamental axioms, postulates, and definitions, as it has so often been represented, but, in addition, it includes in its foundation, facts ascertained by experience, and from the particular cases, general propositions are established. It thus employs Induction as well as Deduction, and is relieved from the charge of being an exclusively deductive science.

In this work, the coördinate and subordinate divisions and the degree of subordination are indicated by the style of numbering.

The principal divisions are marked thus, I, II, III, . . .;

the first subdivisions, thus, **1, 2, 3,** . . .; the second, thus, 1, 2, 3, . . .; the third, thus, 1*st*, 2*d*, 3*d*, . . .; the fourth, thus, *a*, *b*, *c*, . . .; the fifth, thus, α, β, γ, . . .; the sixth, thus, α', β', γ', . . .

Let the teacher see to it that the student not only understands, but that he accurately remembers what he attempts to learn. The rigid exclusion of all extraneous and unnecessary matter, and the systematic arrangement and classification of the principles, will enable the student readily to commit and retain the whole in his memory. His reason will be stimulated by this method; for he will thus have in mind, ready for use, the materials for reflection, the test of truth, and the safeguard against fallacy.

A careful preparation on the part of the teacher, thoroughness of drill and repeated reviews, are indispensable conditions of success in teaching.

As the result of both research and thought, the author submits the work to the enlightened judgment of his fellow-laborers in the great work of education, hoping that it will prove to them a useful auxiliary in imparting a knowledge of this most important science.

A. SCHUYLER.

BALDWIN UNIVERSITY, BEREA, O., *August*, 1869.

INTRODUCTION.

I. INTUITIONS.

1. Definition.

An Intuition is the immediate perception or apprehension of its object. Intuitions are the elements of thought.

The objects of intuitions are the things immediately perceived or apprehended.

2. Classification.

1. Empirical or real intuitions; those whose objects are perceived as contingent, as the attributes of material or spiritual existences.

1*st.* Objective; those which are acquired through the senses, and which pertain to external phenomena.

2*d.* Subjective; those which are acquired by consciousness, and which pertain to mental phenomena.

2. Rational or formal intuitions; those whose objects are apprehended by reason as necessary.

1*st.* Logical; those pertaining to the necessary forms of thought.

2*d.* Mathematical; those pertaining to the necessary relations of quantity.

3. Conditions.

1. Of objective empirical intuitions.
1*st.* Objective conditions; external phenomena.
2*d.* Subjective conditions; the senses—sight, hearing, touch, taste, smell.

2. Of subjective empirical intuitions.
1*st.* Objective conditions; mental phenomena.
2*d.* Subjective condition; consciousness.

3. Of rational intuitions.
1*st.* Objective condition; necessary reality,

a. Absolute, { *α.* Space. *β.* Time.

b. Conditional, { *α.* Substance. *β.* Cause. *γ.* Self-evident relations

2*d.* Subjective condition; reason.

4. Relations of Empirical and Rational Intuitions.

1. Empirical intuitions are the chronological antecedents of rational intuitions; that is, in the order of time, empirical intuitions are the first developed in the intelligence.

2. Rational intuitions are the logical antecedents of empirical intuitions; that is, in the order of nature, the objects of rational intuitions are the necessary conditions of the objects of empirical intuitions.

5. Order of Evolution.

1. Intuitions of concrete objects.
2. Intuitions of relations.

3. Intuitions of relations generalized.
4. Intuitions as related to intellectual processes.
5. Intuitions of the infinite and absolute.

6. Propositions.

1. Intuitions are realities.

Proof.

We are conscious of their existence.

2. Intuitions are valid.

Proofs.

1*st.* The common sense of mankind asserts their validity.

2*d.* They harmonize.

3*d.* They are free from sources of error.

4*th.* If not valid, our faculties are deceptive, and knowledge is impossible.

5*th.* Demonstration implies either an infinite series of dependent propositions or an ultimate basis. But there can be no demonstration by means of an infinite series of dependent propositions; for, to prove one proposition by another, and that by another, and so on, *ad infinitum*, would require infinite time, and is, therefore, impossible. Hence, demonstration implies an ultimate basis. Now, this basis being ultimate, is not derived through any thing else. It must, therefore, be an assumption or an intuition. It can not be an assumption; for then it would not be known to be true, and might be false, and the demonstration would be impossible. The ultimate basis must, therefore, be an intuition, and the validity of demonstration implies the validity of intuitions.

7. Corollaries.

1. The objects of intuitions are realities.
2. The subject of intuitions is a reality.
3. The logical antecedents and consequents of intuitions are valid.

II. THOUGHTS.

1. Definition.

Thought is the recognition of one thing under or in another, as a species under its genus, or a property in its object.

2. Processes.

1. *Conceiving.*	Conceiving is representing a class of objects as contained under the same attribute, or a combination of attributes as contained in the same object.
2. *Judging.*	Judging is recognizing the congruence or confliction of two objects of thought.
3. *Reasoning.*	Reasoning is deriving one judgment from other judgments.

3. Products.

1. *Concepts.*	A concept is the representation of a class of objects as contained under the same attribute, or of a combination of attributes as contained in the same object.

2. *Judgments.* { A judgment is the recognition of the congruence or confliction of two objects of thoughts.

3. *Arguments.* { An argument is the derivation of one judgment from other judgments.

4. Contents.

1. The matter; the objects thought of.

2. The form; the manner of thinking.

1*st.* The contingent forms; the phases that may or may not appear.

2*d.* The necessary forms; the elements that must appear, which are subjective, original, universal, and, therefore, laws.

5. Expression.

1. A term is the expression of a concept in language.

2. A proposition is the expression of a judgment in language.

3. A syllogism is the expression of an argument in language.

III. SCIENCE.

1. Definition.

Science is knowledge classified with respect to principles.

2. Classification.

1. Direct science; science of objects.

1*st.* Science of external phenomena; physical science.

2*d.* Science of internal phenomena; mental science.

2. Reflex science; science of sciences—Logic.

1*st.* Subjective, formal, abstract, or pure logic, which treats of the laws under which the human mind can know; the conditions of knowledge which lie in the nature of thought itself; the relation of thought to its object—the logic of Aristotle.

2*d.* Objective, material, concrete, or applied logic, which treats of the laws under which an object can be known; the conditions of knowledge which lie in the nature of the objects of thought; the relation of the object to the thought—the logic of Bacon.

LOGIC.

I. GENERAL OUTLINE.

1. Definition.

LOGIC is the science which treats of the formal laws of human thought.

2. Exposition.

1. *Its etymology*. The word Logic is derived from λογική an adjective, ἐπιστήμη science, τέχνη art, or πραγματεία investigation, being understood. But λογική is from λόγος, a word ambiguous in its import, denoting both thought and the expression of thought, and thus equivalent both to the Latin *ratio* and *oratio*.

2. *Its genus*. Logic is a science rather than an art.

3. *Its province*. The province of Pure Logic is the formal laws of human thought, both general and special; general, when it treats of the fundamental laws of thought; special, when it treats of the laws applicable to concepts, judgments, or arguments.

3. Classification.

1. In reference to the mind, Logic is classified as

1*st*. Systematic; the complement of doctrines constituting the science. Systematic logic is objective.

2*d.* Habitual; a knowledge of the science and skill in its application. Habitual logic is subjective.

2. In reference to its application, Logic is classified as

1*st.* General or Abstract, which treats of the formal laws of thought without reference to any particular matter, and embraces

a. Pure Logic, which treats of the formal laws of thought as contained, *a priori*, in the nature of the intelligence itself, embracing

α. The doctrine of elements, relating to

α'. The fundamental laws of thought or the universal conditions of the thinkable.

β'. Special laws, relating to concepts, judgments, or arguments.

β. The doctrine of method, relating to

α'. The general laws of method.

β'. Special laws, relating to definition, division, analysis, or proof.

b. Modified Logic, which treats of

α. The nature of truth and error, and the laws of their discrimination.

β. The causes of error and the impediments to the attainment of truth, which are

α'. Physical; disease, hunger, thirst, peculiarities of temperament.

β'. Physico-mental; imperfection in the senses.

γ'. Mental; weakness or derangement of the menta faculties—the intellect, the sensibilities, or the will.

δ'. Circumstantial; education, rank, age, national ıty, social relations, etc.

γ. Aids to correct thinking, embracıng

α'. The acquisition of knowledge, in the various ways.

β'. The communication of knowledge.

2*d*. Special or Applied, the methodology of the various sciences.

II. CONGRUENCE, CONFLICTION, OPPOSITION.

1. Definitions.

1. Concepts that can be united in thought are congruent.

2. Concepts that can not be united in thought are conflictive or opposed. Opposition is of two kinds:

1*st*. Contrary opposition, in which two objects not universally inclusive, are mutually repugnant. Thus, red and blue, walking and standing, etc.

2*d*. Contradictory opposition, in which two objects together are, within their sphere, universally inclusive and mutually repugnant. Thus, red and not-red, walking and not-walking, honest and dishonest within the sphere of moral beings.

2. Classification.

Concepts.
- 1. Congruents.
- 2. Conflictives.
  - 1*st*. Contraries.
  - 2*d*. Contradictories.

3. Formulas.

1. For contraries: *P* is not *Q*.
2. For contradictories: *Non-P* is *Q*.

III. FUNDAMENTAL LAWS OF THOUGHT.

1. The Laws of Identity.

1. *Laws.* — 1*st*. A concept and the sum of all of its elements are totally identical.
2*d*. A concept and a part of its elements are partially identical.

2. *Formulas.* — 1*st*. $C = e+e'+e'' \ldots,$ 2*d*. Some $C = e$, if C denotes the concept, and $e, e', e'', \ldots,$ its elements.

3. *Corollaries.* — 1*st*. C may be substituted for $e+e'+e''+\ldots,$ and conversely.
2*d*. Some C may be substituted for e, and conversely.

2. The Law of Conflictives.

1. *Law.* — Conflictives can not be affirmed of the same object.

2. *Formula.* — S is not both P and Q, if P is not Q, or if *non*-P is Q.

3. *Corollaries.* — 1*st*. If S is P, S is not Q, 2*d*. If S is Q, S is not P, if P is not Q, or *non*-P is Q.

Scholium.—The Law of Conflictives is usually called the Law of Contradiction.

3. The Law of Contradictories.

1. *Law.* — One of two contradictories must be affirmed and the other denied.

2. *Formula.* *S* is either *P* or *Q*, if *non-P* is *Q*.

3. *Corollaries.* — if *non-P* is *Q*.
- 1*st.* If *S* is *P*, *S* is not *Q*,
- 2*d.* If *S* is *Q*, *S* is not *P*,
- 3*d.* If *S* is not *P*, *S* is *Q*,
- 4th. If *S* is not *Q*, *S* is *P*,

Scholium.—The Law of Contradictories is usually called the Law of Excluded Middle.

4. The Law of Reason and Consequent.

1. *Law.*—A reason implies a consequent.

2. *Formula.*—*R* implies C, if *R* is the reason of C.

3. *Corollaries.*
- 1*st.* If *R* is, *C* is.
- 2*d.* If *C* is, some *R* is.
- 3*d.* If every *R* is not, *C* is not.
- 4*th.* If *C* is not, *R* is not.

IV. CONCEPTS.

1. Definition.

A concept is the representation of a class of objects as contained under the same attribute, or of a combination of attributes as contained in the same object. A concept is the product of which conception is the act.

2. Etymology.

Concept, conception, from *concipio* [*con*, *capio*], signifies comprehending many into one.

3. Nature of the Elements.

1. The immediate and irrespective knowledge of an object by intuition.

2. The mediate and relative knowledge of the object as comprising attributes common to it with other objects.

4. Formation.

1. A plurality of objects is furnished by intuition.
2. These objects are compared, their resemblances and differences noted.
3. By attention, the thoughts are directed to the similar and abstracted from the dissimilar.
4. The similar objects are combined into an exclusive object of thought.

5. Relation to Language.

Concepts, in order to become available, must be embodied in a verbal sign.

Language is the product, the instrument, and the embodiment of thought.

6. Characteristics.

1. *Inadequacy.*—A concept is inadequate or incomplete, since but a part of its elements can be represented in thought. Thus, the concept *animal* does not actually represent to the mind all the subordinate classes contained under it. The concept *man* does not represent all the attributes of an individual, since it must represent only the attributes common to all human beings.

2. *Relativity.*—Concepts, as the result of comparison, are necessarily relative. They afford no absolute or irrespective object of knowledge, and can only be realized in consciousness by applying them as terms of

relation to one or more of the objects which agree in certain points of resemblance which they express.

3. *Potential universality.*—A concept can not be represented as a universal in the imagination, for this would require the representation of conflictive attributes as applied to the same object.

A concept is universal, not because it represents, at once, all the objects of a class, but because it may so vary as to represent any.

7. Classification as to Quantity.

1. Extensive concepts are representations of classes of objects as contained under the same attribute.

2. Comprehensive concepts are representations of combinations of attributes as contained in the same object.

8. Extension and Comprehension.

1. The extension of a concept varies inversely as its comprehension; that is, the greater the extension, the less the comprehension, and conversely.

Thus, the concept *animal* is greater, as to extension, than the concept *horse*, since it contains under it the concept horse, as a species, together with a great variety of other species. It is less as to comprehension, since it contains in it, as attributes, those attributes only which are common to all the species contained under it, whereas the concept *horse* contains all the attributes common to all these species, together with what is characteristic of itself.

2. A simple concept, that is, a concept not involving a plurality of attributes, is a maximum as to extension, and a minimum as to comprehension.

Thus the simple concept *being*, which is the highest genus, is a maximum as to extension, since it contains under it all other classes. It is a minimum as to comprehension, since it contains no attribute which is not an attribute of every class and individual contained under it. Hence, it is extensive rather than comprehensive.

3. A simple concept is capable of division, since it can be resolved into classes and individuals.

It is incapable of definition; for an object is defined by referring it to the class immediately containing it, and distinguishing it from other objects of the class by means of its characteristic or differential quality. But the simple concept, or highest genus, is not contained under a higher genus, nor has it a differential quality. It can not, therefore, be defined.

It is incapable of analysis, since it does not contain a plurality of attributes.

4. An individual concept, that is, a concept not involving a plurality of objects, is a minimum as to extension, and a maximum as to comprehension.

Thus, an individual concept, containing no classes or individuals under it, is a minimum as to extension. It is a maximum as to comprehension, since it contains all the attributes common to all the individuals of its class, together with what is characteristic of itself. Hence, it is comprehensive rather than extensive.

5. An individual concept is capable of definition, for it is contained under a class and has a differential quality. It is incapable of division, since it contains nothing under it. It is capable of analysis, since it contains a plurality of attributes.

6. A concept, neither simple nor individual, is neither a maximum nor a minimum, either as to extension or comprehension

Since it is neither the highest genus nor an individual, it is neither a maximum nor a minimum as to extension. Since the higher the genus, the less the comprehension, and the lower the species, the greater the comprehension, it is neither a maximum nor a minimum as to comprehension. Hence, it is both extensive and comprehensive.

7. A concept neither simple nor individual is capable of definition, since it is contained under a class, and has a differential quality. It is capable of division, since it contains either classes or individuals under it. It is capable of analysis, since it contains a plurality of attributes.

9. Classification as to Quality.

1. Clear concepts are those which are discriminated, as a whole, from other concepts. Clearness is attained by definition.

2. Obscure concepts are those which are confounded with other concepts.

Obscureness is avoided by definition.

3. Distinct concepts are those in which the classes or individuals contained under them, or the attributes contained in them, are discriminated.

Extensive distinctness is attained by division, comprehensive distinctness is attained by analysis.

4. Indistinct concepts are those in which the classes or individuals contained under them, or the attributes contained in them, are confounded.

10. Qualities involved in Distinctness.

1. A clear apprehension of the classes or individuals contained under the concept, or of the attributes contained in it.

2. A clear discrimination of these classes or individuals and attributes.

3. A clear recognition of the nexus which binds these classes or individuals and attributes into unity.

11. Concepts admitting Extensive or Comprehensive Distinctness.

1. Simple concepts are capable of extensive, but incapable of comprehensive, distinctness.

2. Individual concepts are capable of comprehensive, but incapable of extensive, distinctness.

3. Concepts, neither simple nor individual, are capable both of extensive and comprehensive distinctness.

12. Specific Rules for attaining Distinctness.

1. Seek for the positive elements; the negative may be sought for as aids in determining the positive.

2. Among the positive elements, seek out the intrinsic and permanent in preference to the extrinsic and transitory.

3. Among the intrinsic and permanent, seek out the necessary and essential, then descend to the contingent and accidental.

13. Sources of Indistinctness.

1. The nature of the concept itself, which is multiplicity, bound, by a mental process, into unity.

2. The dependence of the concept on language as the condition of its continuance.

14. Remedy for Indistinctness.

The remedy for indistinctness is the rules for distinctness.

15. Classification as to Validity.

1. Valid concepts are those which embrace only intuitions, or intuitions with their logical antecedents and consequents. Valid concepts are true.

2. Invalid concepts are those which embrace assumed elements. Invalid concepts may be true or false.

16. Classification as to Truth.

1. True concepts are those which correspond to their objects. True concepts may be valid or invalid.

2. False concepts are those which do not correspond to their objects. False concepts are invalid.

17. Classification as to Congruity.

1. Congruous concepts are those in which all of the elements harmonize.

Congruity depends on the nexus which binds the elements together into unity.

2. Incongruous concepts are those which embrace conflictive elements,—contraries or contradictories.

Incongruity is the mark of invalidity and indicates that some elements have been assumed without warrant.

18. Classification as to Completeness.

1. Complete concepts are those which embrace all of the elements of their objects.

Completeness is, in general, an ideal perfection. Very few, if any, of our concepts are complete.

2. Incomplete concepts are those which embrace only a part of the elements of their objects.

Incompleteness characterizes most, if not all, of our concepts. Most objects have qualities which have escaped our observation. Different persons form different concepts of the same objects, one combining one set of elements, another, another set.

19. Classification as to their Relations in Extension.

1. *Of Inclusion.*—One concept is included in another when the sphere of the former is contained in the sphere of the latter.

There are two cases of inclusion:

1*st.* *Of Subordination.*—One concept is subordinate to another when the former is contained under the latter as a species under a genus, or as an individual under a species. Thus, the concept *horse* is subordinate to the concept *quadruped*, since *horse* is a *species* of which *quadruped* is the *genus*. The concept *George Washington* is subordinate to the concept *man*, since *George Washington* is an *individual* of which *man* is the *species*.

If one concept is subordinate to another, it is subordinate to any higher concept. Thus, since the species *horse* is subordinate to the genus *quadruped*, it is subordinate to any higher genus, as *animal*, *organized being*, *being*.

2*d.* *Of Coextension.*—One concept is coextensive with another when they have a common sphere.

Thus, equilateral triangles are coextensive with equiangular triangles, since they have a common sphere, that is, since every equilateral triangle is equiangular, and every equiangular triangle is equilateral.

2. *Of Exclusion.*—One concept is excluded from another when their spheres have no part common.

There are two cases of exclusion:

1*st.* *Of Coördination.*—Two concepts are coördinate

when they are exclusive and both immediately comprehended under the same concept. Thus, the concepts *horse* and *sheep* are coördinate, since they are exclusive, and both immediately subordinate, as species, to the genus *quadruped.*

2*d.* *Of Non-coördination.*—Two exclusive concepts are non-coördinate when they are not immediately subordinate to the same concept. Thus, the concepts *Arabian horse* and *sheep* are non-coördinate, since *Arabian horse* is a species of the genus *horse*, while *sheep* is not.

3. *Of Intersection.*—Two concepts intersect when their spheres have a common part, and each, a part not common. Thus, the concepts *men* and *liars* intersect, since some men are liars and some liars are men, some men are not liars and some liars are not men.

20. Notation expressing these Relations.

1. The relation of subordination may be expressed by one circle within another, the larger circle expressing the superior concept, the smaller, an inferior.

Thus, 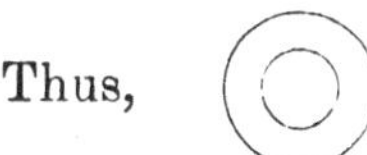

2. The relation of coextension may be expressed by two equal coincident circles.

Thus, 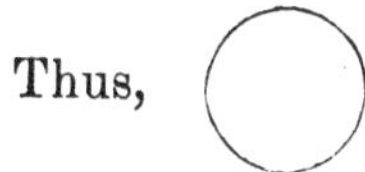

3. The relation of coördination may be expressed by two equal exclusive circles both contained within a larger circle. The larger circle expresses the superior

concept, the smaller circles express coördinate inferior concepts.

Thus, 

4. The relation of exclusive non-coördination may be expressed by one of two circles within, and the other without, a third circle.

Thus, 

5. The relation of intersection may be expressed by two intersecting circles.

Thus, 

21. Summary of the Relations of Extensive Concepts.

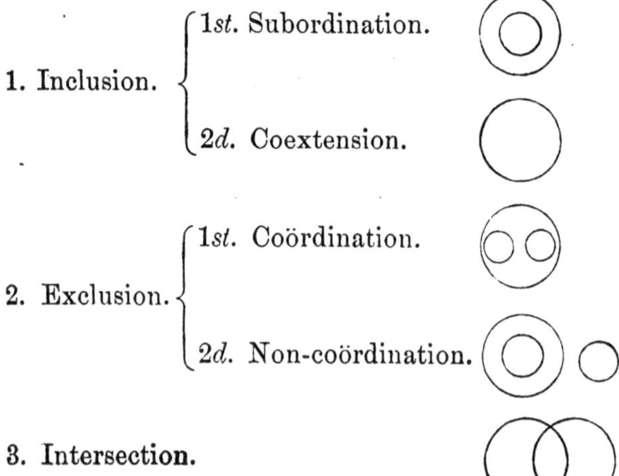

22. The Laws of Classification by Genera and Species.

1. *The Law of Homogeneity.*—However different two concepts, neither of which is the highest genus, both are subordinate to the same higher concept, though not necessarily coördinate with each other; for, ultimately, every concept may be referred to that of *being*, the highest genus. Hence, things the most dissimilar, must, in certain respects, be similar.

2. *The Law of Heterogeneity.*—Every concept contains other concepts under it. In thought, therefore, the division of concepts gives concepts, not individuals. Hence, things the most similar must, in certain respects, be dissimilar. Thus, take any two concepts with a small difference. Now, this difference can be divided, thus giving new concepts distinguished by this partial difference, and so on, *ad infinitum*. But the infinite divisibility of concepts, like the infinite divisibility of space, time, and matter, exists only in speculation.

To illustrate, let us classify angles thus:

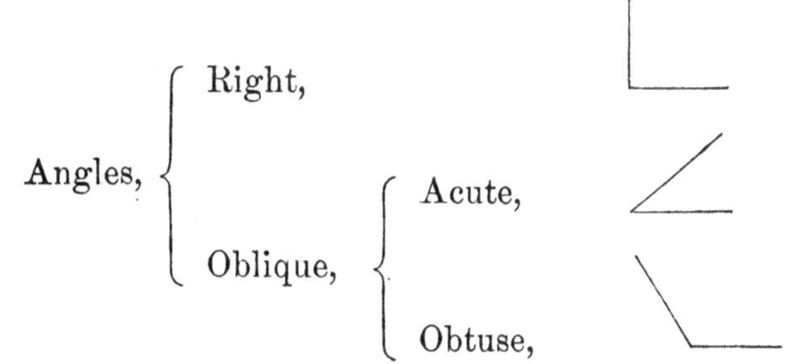

Here we pause, not because it is impossible to pursue the classification farther, but because it is not called for. But we can conceive these angles situated in a horizontal, a vertical, or an oblique plane, giving horizontal, vertical, or oblique angles, and these angles may have any position in these planes, and the sides may take an infinite number of directions, for each position of the vertex, and the acute angle may vary through an infinite number of states between the limits 0 and 90°, and the obtuse angle may vary, in like manner, between the limits 90° and 180°.

23. Classification as to Relations in Comprehension.

1. *As to Identity.*

- 1*st*. Identical.
  - *a*. Absolutely identical.
  - *b*. Relatively identical.
    - *α*. Reciprocating or convertible.
    - *β*. Similar or cognate.
- 2*d*. Different.
  - *a*. Absolutely different.
  - *b*. Relatively different.

2. *As to Congruence.*

- 1*st*. Congruent.
- 2*d*. Conflictive.
  - *a*. Contrary.
  - *b*. Contradictory.

3. *As to Elements.*

1*st*. Intrinsic; those formed of essential elements.
2*d*. Extrinsic; those formed of accidental elements.

4. *As to Proximate Relations.*

1*st*. *Of Involution.*—One concept is involved in another, when the first forms a part of the sum-total of the elements which together constitute the comprehension of the second. Thus, the sides, angles, and area are involved in the concept, triangle.

2*d.* *Coördination.*—Two concepts are coördinate when they are exclusive, and both immediately comprehended, as elements, of the same concept. Thus, the sides and angles of a triangle are coördinate.

V. JUDGMENTS.

1. Definition.

A judgment is the recognition of the congruence or confliction of two objects of thought.

2. Expression.

A proposition is the expression of a judgment in language. Thus, *S* is *P*.

3. Elements.

1. The concepts.
   - 1*st.* The subject, or determined concept—*S*.
   - 2*d.* The predicate, or determining concept—*P*.

2. The relation of the concepts—in the copula, *is*.

4. Concepts and Judgments compared.

1. A concept may be regarded as an implicit or undeveloped judgment.

2. A judgment may be regarded as an explicit or developed concept.

5. Classification as to Origin.

1. Primitive.
   - 1*st*. Assumptive.
   - 2*d*. Intuitive.
     - *a*. The predicate the logical antecedent of the subject.
     - *b*. The predicate an essential attribute of the subject.
2. Derivative.
   - 1*st*. Problematical.
   - 2*d*. Demonstrative.

6. Classification as to Validity.

1. Valid.
   - 1*st*. When the concepts are valid, and
   - 2*d*. The relation of the concepts is
     - *a*. Intuitive, or
     - *b*. Demonstrative.
2. Invalid; when the laws of validity are violated.

7. Classification as to Truth.

1. True; when the relation expressed corresponds to the reality.
2. False; when the relation expressed does not correspond to the reality.

8. Classification as to Extension and Comprehension.

1. A judgment is extensive when the determining predicate is considered as the whole of extension containing the subject. Thus, man is an animal.

2. A judgment is comprehensive when the determined subject is considered as the whole of comprehension containing the predicate. Thus, man is mortal.

9. Classification as to Form.

1. A categorical judgment is one in which the relation of the subject and predicate is unqualified by a condition. Thus, *S* is *P*.

2. A conditional judgment is one in which the relation of the subject and predicate is qualified by a condition.

Conditional judgments are of three varieties:

1*st*. Hypothetical, when the qualifying condition is an hypothesis. Thus, if *S* is *P*, *T* is *U*.

2*d*. Disjunctive, when the qualifying condition is a disjunction. Thus, *S* is either *P* or *Q*.

3*d*. Dilemmatic, when the qualifying condition is both an hypothesis and a disjunction. Thus, if *S* is *P*, *T* is either *U* or *V*.

10. Classification as to Quantity.

1. Universal. { All *S* is *P*. / No *S* is *P*. }

2. Particular. { Some *S* is *P*. / Some *S* is not *P*. }

11. Classification as to Quality.

1. Affirmative. { All *S* is *P*. / Some S is *P*. }

2. Negative. { No *S* is *P*. / Some *S* is not *P*. }

12. Principles of Expression.

1. *Principles warranting Affirmation.*

1*st*. Immediate.

a. Principles.—The Laws of Identity.

b. Formula.—*S* is *P*, if *S* and *P* are identical, either *α*. Totally, or *β*. Partially.

2*d*. Mediate.

a. Principle.—The Law of Contradictories.

b. Formulas. { *α*. *S* is *P*, if *S* is not *Q*, / *β*. *S* is *Q*, if *S* is not *P*, } if *non-P* is *Q*.

2. *Principles warranting Negation.*

1*st*. Immediate.

a. Principle.—The Law of Conflictives.

b. Formula.—*P* is not *Q*, if *P* and *Q* are conflictives.

2*d*. Mediate.

a. Principle.—The Law of Conflictives.

b. Formulas. { *α*. *S* is not *P*, if *S* is *Q*, / *β*. *S* is not *Q*, if *S* is *P*, } if *P* is not *Q*, or *non-P* is *Q*.

3. *Principle warranting Hypothecation.*

1*st*. Principle—The Law of Reason and Consequent.

2*d*. Formula—If *R* is, *C* is, if *R* is the reason of *C*.

4. *Principle warranting Disjunction.*

1*st*. Principle.—The Law of Contradictories.

2*d*. Formula. { *S* is either *P* or *Q*, if *P* and *Q* are contradictories.

13. Classification of Categorical Judgments.

1. Universal. { 1*st*. Affirmative. (A) All *S* is *P*.
   2*d*. Negative. (E) No *S* is *P*.

2. Particular. { 1*st*. Affirmative. (I) Some *S* is *P*.
   2*d*. Negative. (O) Some *S* is not *P*.

14. Laws of Validity.

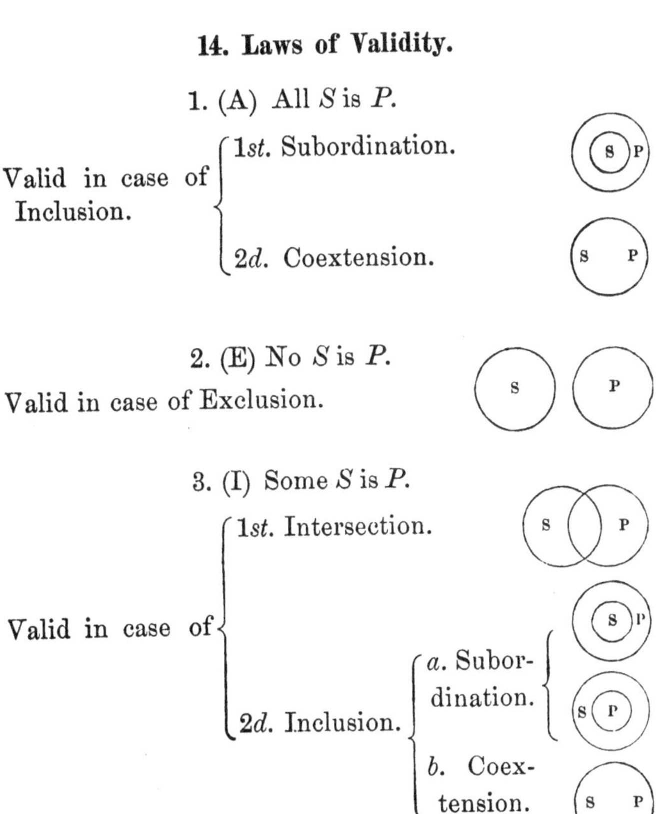

1. (A) All *S* is *P*.

Valid in case of Inclusion. { 1*st*. Subordination. / 2*d*. Coextension.

2. (E) No *S* is *P*.

Valid in case of Exclusion.

3. (I) Some *S* is *P*.

Valid in case of { 1*st*. Intersection. / 2*d*. Inclusion. { *a*. Subordination. / *b*. Coextension.

4. (O) Some S is not P.

Valid in case of
- 1*st*. Intersection.
- 2*d*. Inclusion—Subordination.
- 3*d*. Exclusion.

15. Opposition.

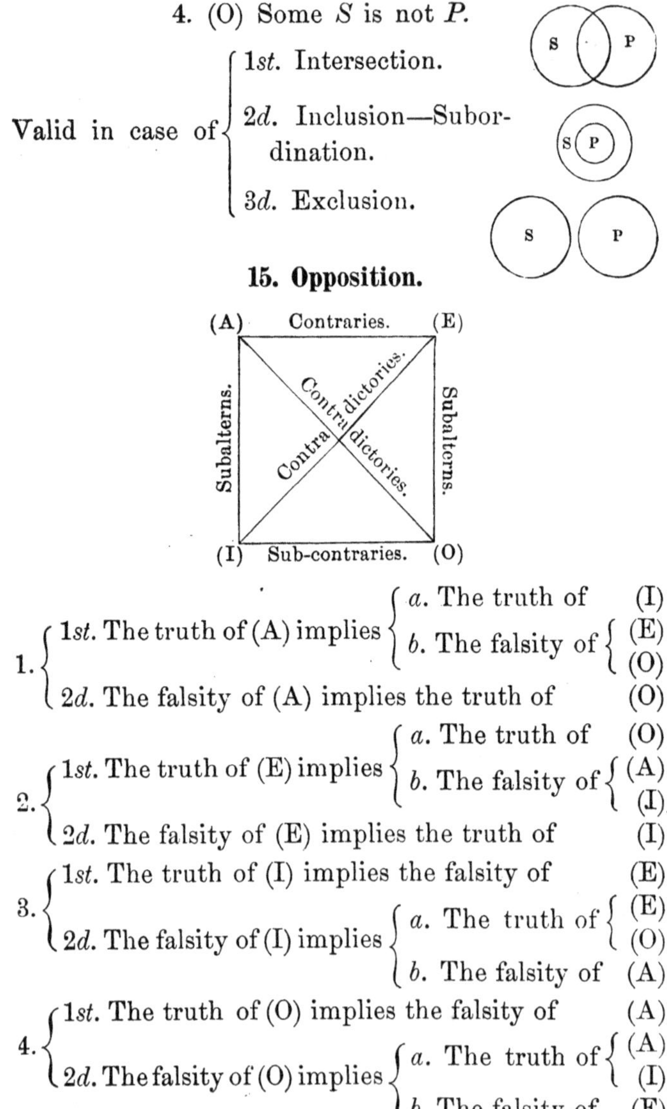

1.
- 1*st*. The truth of (A) implies
  - *a*. The truth of (I)
  - *b*. The falsity of (E) (O)
- 2*d*. The falsity of (A) implies the truth of (O)

2.
- 1*st*. The truth of (E) implies
  - *a*. The truth of (O)
  - *b*. The falsity of (A) (I)
- 2*d*. The falsity of (E) implies the truth of (I)

3.
- 1*st*. The truth of (I) implies the falsity of (E)
- 2*d*. The falsity of (I) implies
  - *a*. The truth of (E) (O)
  - *b*. The falsity of (A)

4.
- 1*st*. The truth of (O) implies the falsity of (A)
- 2*d*. The falsity of (O) implies
  - *a*. The truth of (A) (I)
  - *b*. The falsity of (E)

16. The Laws of Opposition.

1. The truth of a universal implies the truth of its particular.

2. The falsity of a universal does not imply the falsity of its particular.

3. The falsity of a particular implies the falsity of its universal.

4. The truth of a particular does not imply the truth of its universal.

5. The contraries can not be both true, but may be both false.

6. The sub-contraries can not be both false, but may be both true.

7. Two contradictories can not be both true or both false.

17. Distribution of the Concepts of a Judgment.

1. *Definitions.*

1*st*. A concept is distributed when all of it is taken.

2*d*. A concept is undistributed when only a part of it is taken.

2. *Principles.*

1*st*. All universals distribute the subject.

2*d*. All negatives distribute the predicate.

3*d*. No particular distributes the subject.

4*th*. An affirmative may or may not distribute the predicate.

3. *Consequences.*

1*st*. (A) distributes the subject, and may distribute the predicate.

2*d*. (E) distributes both the subject and predicate.

3*d*. (I) does not distribute the subject, but may distribute the predicate.

4*th*. (O) distributes the predicate, but not the subject.

4. *Remarks.*

1*st*. (A) distributes the predicate in case S and P are coextensive. In this case, all S is all P, and all P is all S. This relation holds true in case of definitions, equations, identical propositions, and when S and P designate, by different attributes, the same class not susceptible of subdivision. Thus, All equilateral triangles are equiangular, and All equiangular triangles are equilateral.

2*d*. (I) distributes the predicate in case S is the genus of which P is a species, or in case S is the species of which P is an individual. Thus, Some animals are all horses.

3*d*. Both (E) and (O) distribute the predicate. Thus, No S is P means Any S is not any P. Some S is not P means Some S is not any P.

4*th*. For those cases in which the predicate of a negative is, by an express statement, undistributed, see Hamilton's Classification of Propositions.

18. Conversion.

1. *Definition.*

The converse of a proposition is the proposition obtained by transposing the terms of the original proposition. Thus, the converse of S is P is P is S.

2. *Kinds.*

1*st*. *Simple conversion*, when the converse has the same quantity and quality as the original proposition.

a. (E) may always be converted simply.

Thus, (E) No S is P. (E) No P is S.

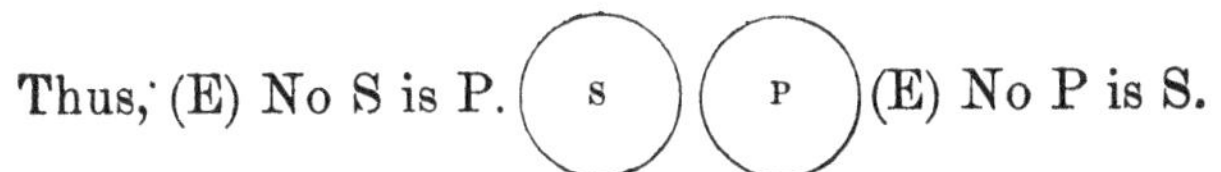

b. (I) may always be converted simply. Thus,

(I) Some S is P.

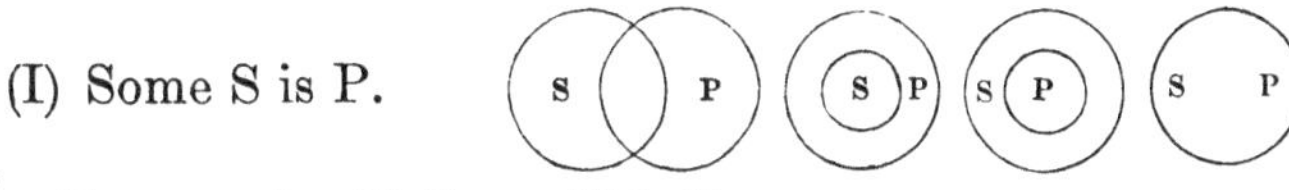

Conversely, (I) Some P is S.

c. (A) may be converted simply when S and P are coextensive.

Thus, (A) All S is P. (S P) (A) All P is S.

d. (A) may always be changed to (E) which may be converted simply. Thus,

(A) All S is P = (E) No S is non-P. (S) P (S P)

Conversely, (E) No non-P is S.

e. (O) may be changed to (I) which may be converted simply.

Thus, (O) Some S is not P = (I) Some S is non-P.

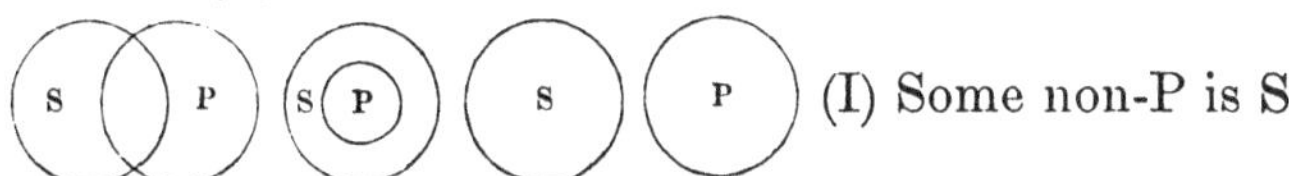

(I) Some non-P is S

2*d.* *Conversion by limitation,* when the quantity is reduced in the converse.

a. (A) may always be converted by limitation.

Thus, (A) All S is P. (I) Some P is S.

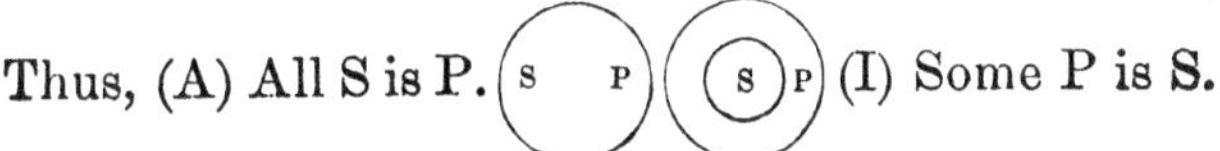

b. (E) may always be converted by limitation.

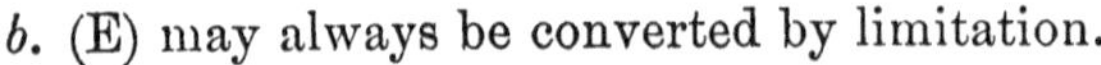

Thus, (E) No S is P. (O) Some P is not S.

c. (E) may always be changed into A, which may be converted by limitation.

Thus, (E) No S is P = (A) All S is non-P. (I) Some non-P is S.

19. Classification of Hypothetical Judgments.

Forms.	*Laws of Validity.*
1. If A is B, A is C.	If B is C.
2. If A is B, A is not C.	If no B is C.
3. If A is not B, A is C.	If B and C are contradictories.
4. If A is not B, A is not C.	If C is B.
5. If A is B, B is C.	If A is C and coextensive with B.
6. If A is B, B is not C	If A is not C and coextensive with B.
7. If A is not B, B is C.	If A and C are contradictories.

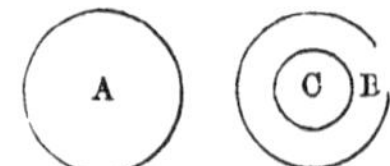

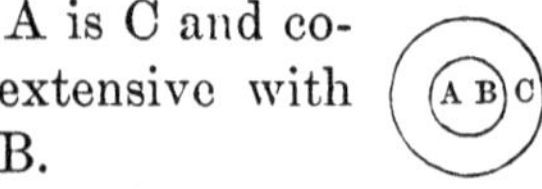

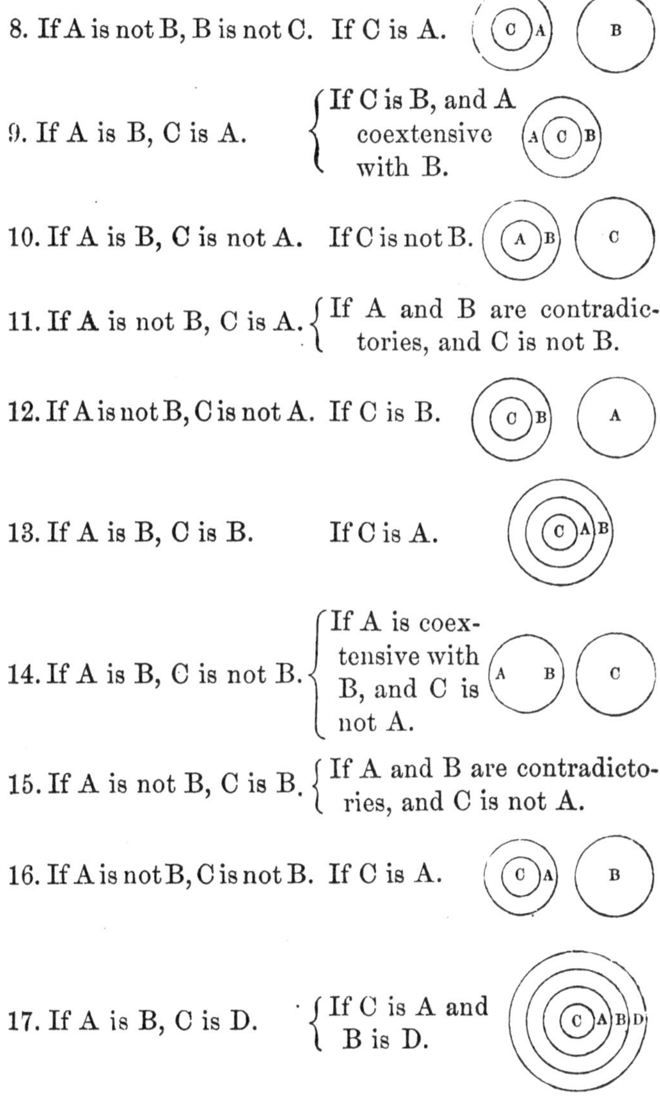

8. If A is not B, B is not C. If C is A.

9. If A is B, C is A. If C is B, and A coextensive with B.

10. If A is B, C is not A. If C is not B.

11. If A is not B, C is A. If A and B are contradictories, and C is not B.

12. If A is not B, C is not A. If C is B.

13. If A is B, C is B. If C is A.

14. If A is B, C is not B. If A is coextensive with B, and C is not A.

15. If A is not B, C is B. If A and B are contradictories, and C is not A.

16. If A is not B, C is not B. If C is A.

17. If A is B, C is D. If C is A and B is D.

18. If A is B, C is not D. { If C is A and B is not D.

19. If A is not B, C is D. { If A is B and C is D are contradictory propositions.

20. If A is not B, C is not D. { If C is A and D is B.

20. Classification of Disjunctive Judgments.

The judgment, S is P or Q, may be

1. *Divisive.* Thus, Angles are right or oblique; that is, angles are divided into right angles and oblique angles.

2. *Disjunctive in expression.* Thus, This electricity is vitreous or positive—these terms denoting the same kind of electricity.

3. *Disjunctive in thought.* Thus, The animal is a vertebrate or an invertebrate.

The first and second classes are disjunctive only in form, but categorical in sense. The third class only is logically disjunctive. This disjunction may be

1*st.* *In the copula.* Thus, S either is or is not P. This is pure contradictory opposition, and the judgment is valid by the Law of Contradictories.

2*d.* *In the terms.* Thus, S is either P or Q. In this case, there are two varieties:

a. When P and Q are contraries. We then have contrary opposition, and can not affirm *a priori*, but only *a posteriori*, that S is either P or Q.

In contrary opposition, the judgment, S is either P or Q, is valid on the condition that all suppositions contrary to it are shown to be false. Then,

If S is P, S is not Q; if S is Q, S is not P;
If S is not P, S is Q; if S is not Q, S is P.

b. When P and Q are contradictories. We then have contradictory opposition and the judgment is valid by the Law of Contradictories.

The disjunction may lie in the subject as well as in the predicate, when the disjunction is in the terms.

21. Classification of Logical Disjunctives.

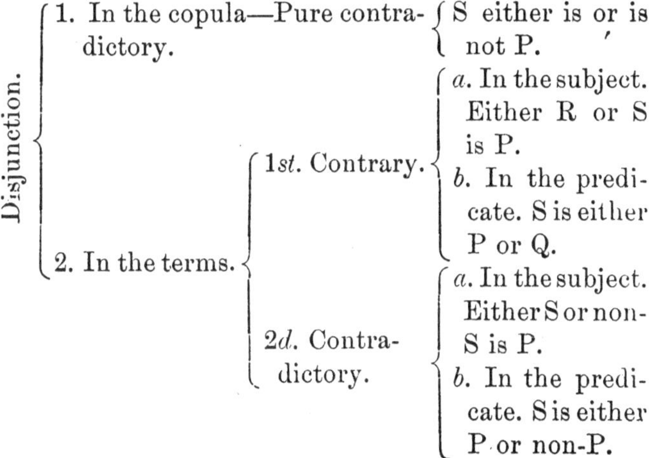

22. Classification of Dilemmatic Judgments.

1.
1. If A is B, S is either P or Q.
2. If A is B, S is neither P nor Q.
3. If A is not B, S is either P or Q.
4. If A is not B, S is neither P nor Q.

2.
5. If either A is B or C is D, S is either P or Q.
6. If either A is B or C is D, S is neither P nor Q.
7. If neither A is B nor C is D, S is either P or Q.
8. If neither A is B nor C is D, S is neither P nor Q

The disjunctive consequent is in contrary opposition, for, if in contradictory opposition, the consequents of 1, 3, 5, and 7 would be true, and the consequents of 2, 4, 6, and 8 would be false, by the Law of Contradictories, and the reason in the conditional clause would be redundant. Thus, it would be superfluous to say, If A is B, S is either P or non-P; for S is either P or non-P, whether A is B or not.

VI. ARGUMENTS.

Definition.

An argument is the derivation of a judgment from another judgment or from other judgments.

1. IMMEDIATE ARGUMENTS.

1. Definition.

An immediate argument is an argument in which the relation of the concepts of the derived judgment is inferred from another judgment or from other judgments without the intervention of a middle concept

2. Varieties.

1. Inferences from opposition. [V. 15.]
2. Inferences from conversion. [V. 18.]
3. Inferences from modal restriction.

Thus, S is necessarily P, ∴ S is actually P, ∴ S is probably P, ∴ S is possibly P.

4. Inferences from composition.

Thus, A is in C, B is in C, ∴ A and B are in C.

5. Inferences from divisive judgments.

Thus, S is P, Q, or R, ∴
- *1st.* The P of S is neither the Q nor the R of S.
- *2d.* The non-P of S is either the Q or the R of S.
- *3d.* The neither P nor Q of S is the R of S.

6. Inferences by means of privatives.

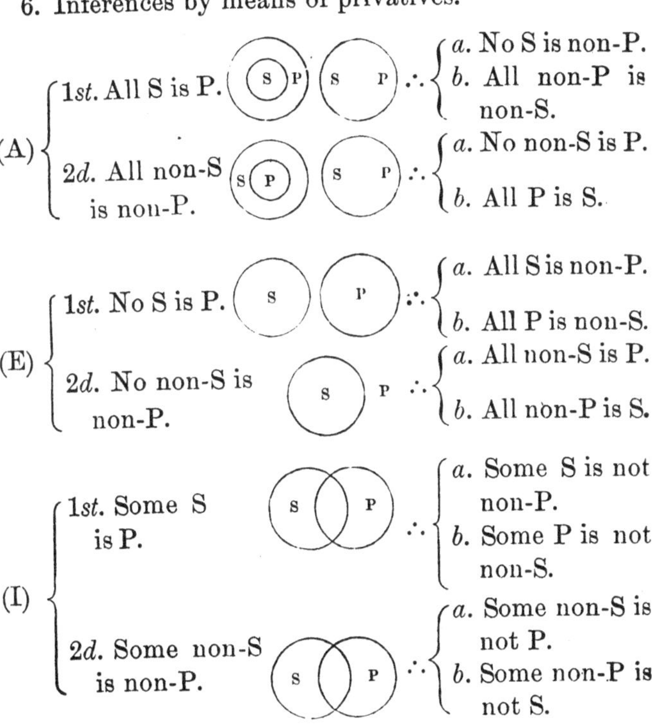

(A)
- *1st.* All S is P. ∴ *a.* No S is non-P. *b.* All non-P is non-S.
- *2d.* All non-S is non-P. ∴ *a.* No non-S is P. *b.* All P is S.

(E)
- *1st.* No S is P. ∴ *a.* All S is non-P. *b.* All P is non-S.
- *2d.* No non-S is non-P. ∴ *a.* All non-S is P. *b.* All non-P is S.

(I)
- *1st.* Some S is P. ∴ *a.* Some S is not non-P. *b.* Some P is not non-S.
- *2d.* Some non-S is non-P. ∴ *a.* Some non-S is not P. *b.* Some non-P is not S.

(O)

1*st*. Some S is not P. 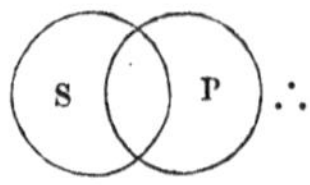

∴ *a*. Some S is non-P.
b. Some non-P is not non-S.

2*d*. Some non-S is not non-P. 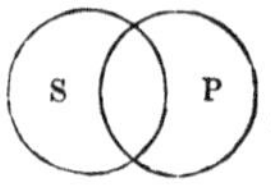

∴ *a*. Some non-S is P.
b. Some P is not S.

2. MEDIATE ARGUMENTS.

1. Definitions.

1. A mediate argument is an argument in which the relation of the concepts of the derived judgment is inferred from other judgments through the intervention of a middle concept.

2. The derived judgment is called the conclusion.

3. The judgments from which the derived judgment is inferred are called the premises.

2. Expression.

A syllogism is the expression of an argument.

Thus, { All M is P. / All S is M. / ∴ All S is P. } Hence, a syllogism contains

1. Three terms.
   - 1*st*. The extremes.
     - *a*. The major term (P), the predicate of the conclusion.
     - *b*. The minor term (S), the subject of the conclusion.
   - 2*d*. The middle term (M), the medium of comparison.

2. Three propositions.
   - 1st. The premises.
     - a. The major premise in which (M) and (P) are compared.
     - b. The minor premise in which (S) and (M) are compared.
   - 2d. The conclusion in which the relation of (S) and (P) is inferred.

3. Illustration.

Every responsible agent is a free agent.
Man is a responsible agent.
∴ Man is a free agent.

The subject, man, and the predicate, a free agent, of the conclusion, Man is a free agent, are the extremes, of which the predicate, a free agent, is the major term, and the subject, man, is the minor term.

The term, responsible agent, with which the extremes are separately compared in the premises, is the middle term.

The premise, Every responsible agent is a free agent, in which the middle term is compared with the major term, is the major premise.

The premise, Man is a responsible agent, in which the minor term is compared with the middle, is the minor premise.

The middle term is found in each of the premises, but not in the conclusion.

One extreme is found in one premise, the other in the other, and both in the conclusion.

Let us now consider this argument, as an argument,

1. *In extensive quantity.* In this case, the concept, responsible agent, is contained under the concept,

free agent; that is, the class of responsible agents is a species of which the class of free agents is the genus.

The concept, man, is contained under the concept, responsible agent; that is, the class, man, is a species of which the class of responsible agents is the genus.

Hence, on the principle, that a part of a part is a part of the whole, the concept, man, is contained under the concept free agent.

In extensive quantity, the copula, *is*, signifies *is contained under*.

Let us now generalize and symbolize this argument, thus:

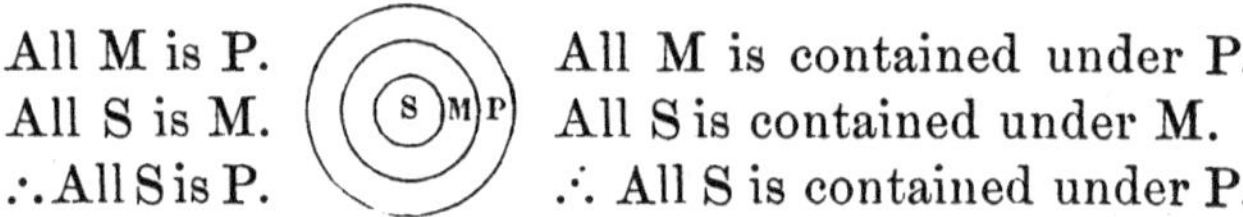

All M is P.
All S is M.
∴ All S is P.

All M is contained under P.
All S is contained under M.
∴ All S is contained under P.

2. *In comprehensive quantity.* In this case, the concept, responsible agent, contains in it, that is, comprehends, the concept, free agent, as one of its attributes.

The concept, man, comprehends the concept, responsible agent, as one of its attributes.

Hence, on the principle that the whole comprehends a part of a part, the concept, man, comprehends the concept, free agent.

In comprehensive quantity, the copula, *is*, signifies *comprehends*.

Let us now generalize and symbolize this argument, transposing the premises, thus:

S comprehends M.
M comprehends P.
∴ S comprehends P.

It is to be observed that S, which is the least in extensive quantity, is the greatest in comprehensive quantity, and that P, which is the greatest in extensive quantity, is the least in comprehensive quantity.

The names, major and minor terms, as defined, are significant only in extensive quantity, and even in this quantity, not always. The major term, as a matter of fact, is frequently less in extension than the minor term. They are, therefore, to be regarded as mere technical expressions, the major term denoting the predicate of the conclusion, and the minor, the subject.

The expressions, major and minor premises, are also to be regarded as technical expressions, the major premise being the premise containing the major term, the minor premise, the premise containing the minor term.

The order of the premises is not essential, though the major premise generally stands first. The conclusion may even be placed before the premises.

4. Remarks on Mediate Arguments.

1. The function of an argument is to prove that a certain relation exists between two concepts, when that relation is not self-evident.

In mediate arguments, this is accomplished by selecting, as the medium of comparison, a third concept, called, for this reason, the middle concept, with which the other concepts are separately compared.

The separate relations of the extremes to the middle prove their relations to each other.

2. The conclusion must not only be compatible with

the premises, but must be necessitated by them, otherwise the argument is a fallacy, thus:

No P is M.
No S is M.
∴ No S is P.

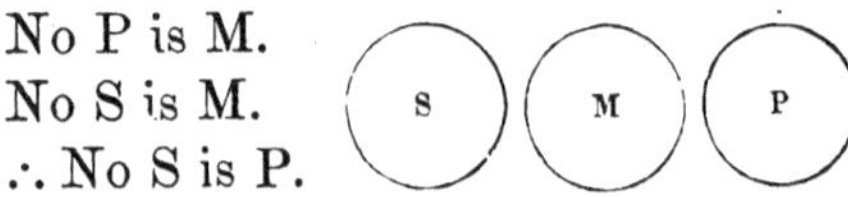

Now, though this conclusion may be true, as a fact, the premises do not prove it; for we might have the same premises and a contrary conclusion, thus:

No P is M.
No S is M.
∴ All S is P.

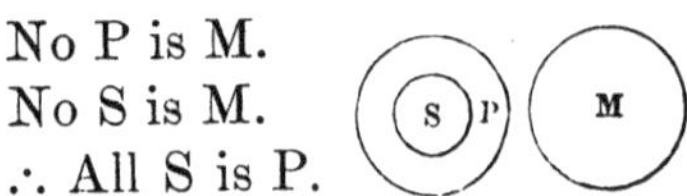

But this argument, like the other, is invalid, though the conclusion is true; for the premises do not necessitate the conclusion.

3. The same relation may have different expressions, thus:

No P is M.
All S is M.
∴ No S is P.

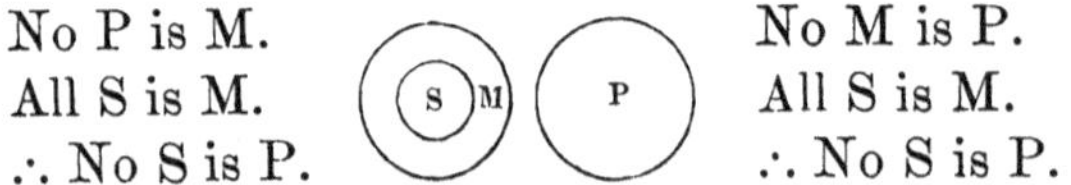

No M is P.
All S is M.
∴ No S is P.

These arguments are identical in thought, as is seen by the figures, with an accidental difference of expression.

5. Laws warranting the Conclusions.

(A), (E), (I), (O).

To prove (A). { All M is P. All S is M. ∴ All S is P. }

S M P

Hence, a universal affirmative conclusion is warranted, if all of the middle is contained under the predicate and all of the subject, under the middle.

To prove (E).

All P is M.
No S is M.
∴ No S is P.

All S is M.
No P is M.
∴ No S is P.

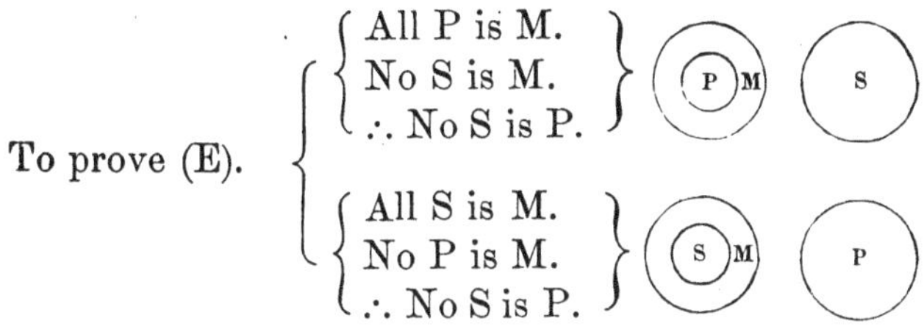

Hence, a universal negative conclusion is warranted, if all of one extreme, and none of the other, is contained under the middle.

To prove (I).

All M is P.
All M is S.
∴ Some S is P.

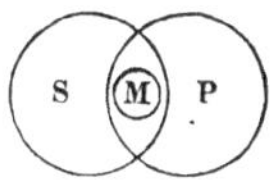

All M is P.
Some M is S.
∴ Some S is P.

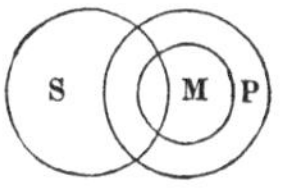

All M is S.
Some M is P.
∴ Some S is P.

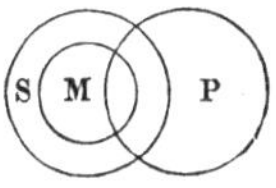

Hence, a particular affirmative conclusion is warranted,

1*st.* If all of the middle is contained under each extreme.

2*d.* If all of the middle is contained under one extreme and a part of it, under the other.

In both cases, the same thing—either all or the same part of the middle—is contained under both extremes; hence, the extremes must, in part, at least, coincide

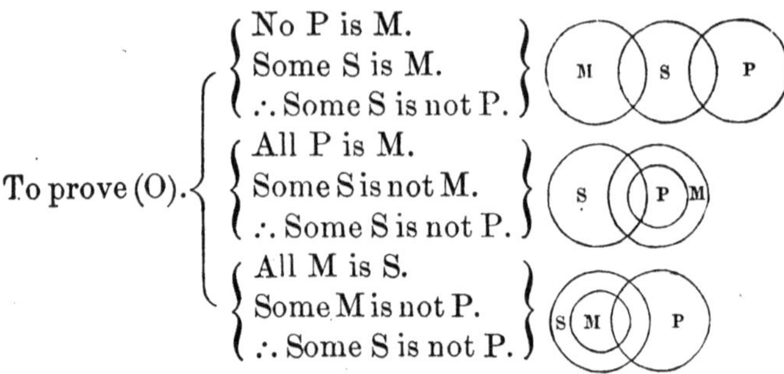

Hence, a particular negative conclusion is warranted,

1*st*. If all of the predicate is excluded from the middle and some of the subject is contained under the middle.

2*d*. If all of the predicate is contained under the middle and some of the subject is excluded from the middle.

3*d*. If all of the middle is contained under the subject and some of the middle is excluded from the predicate.

In all these cases, the extremes are so related to the middle that some of the subject is excluded from the predicate.

6. Formal Fallacies.

1. *Undistributed Middle.*

It has already been stated that all universals distribute the subject, and all negatives the predicate, that no particular distributes the subject, and that an affirmative may or may not distribute the predicate.

(A) distributes the predicate in case S is coextensive with P, which is the case in definitions, equations, identical propositions, etc.

(I) distributes the predicate in case S includes P, that is, when S is the genus and P the species.

In all other cases, the predicate of (A) or (I) is undistributed.

Let us now take an argument with an undistributed middle:

All P is M.
All S is M.
∴ All S is P.

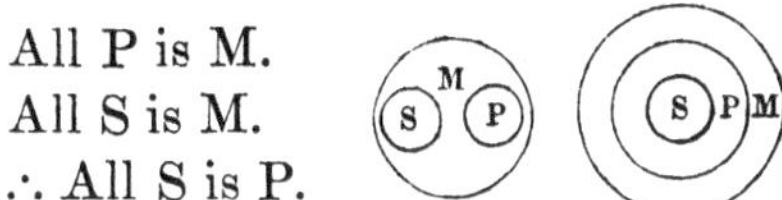

The conclusion does not necessarily follow from the premises, though it may be accidentally true, as seen in the second diagram above.

Let now the major premise be a case of coextension, then M will be distributed and the argument valid.

All P is M.
All S is M.
∴ All S is P.

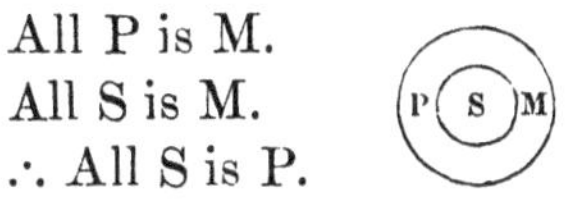

We frequently meet with such reasonings in scientific works. The following, the conclusiveness of which is unquestioned, is a specimen taken from geometry:

Similar polygons are those which are equiangular and have their corresponding sides proportional.

Regular polygons of the same number of sides are equiangular and have their corresponding sides proportional.

∴ Regular polygons of the same number of sides are similar polygons.

The major premise is a definition of similar polygons, and, consequently, its subject and predicate are coextensive, and the predicate distributed.

The minor premise is a demonstrated proposition. The reasoning is valid, and the conclusion true.

Again, take the following:

S = M.
P = M.
∴ S = P.

Let the minor premise be a case of coextension.

All P is M.
All S is M.
∴ Some S is P.

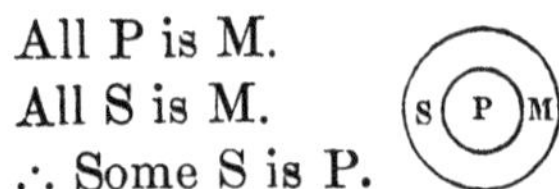

Let us take another argument with an undistributed middle:

All P is M.
Some S is M.
∴ Some S is P.

The conclusion is not necessarily true, but may be accidentally true, as seen above.

Let the major premise be a case of coextension.

All P is M.
Some S is M.
∴ Some S is P.

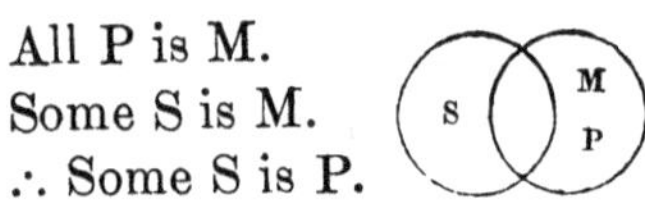

Let the minor premise be a case in which S includes M, thus:

All P is M.
Some S is M.
∴ Some S is P.

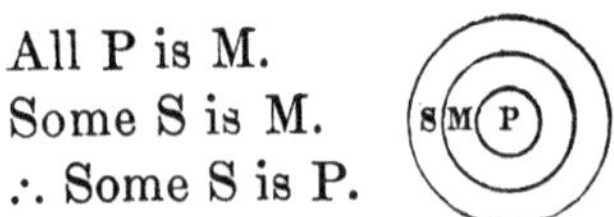

Hence, if the middle term is undistributed, no conclusion is warranted; but it will suffice if the middle term is distributed in one of the premises.

The fallacy of the undistributed middle consists in the fact that but a part of the middle is compared with the extremes in the two premises, and it is not certain that it is the same part. The extremes, then, are not known to be compared with the same thing, and there is no warrant for inferring their relations to each other.

2. *Illicit Process.*

An illicit process consists in distributing either the major or the minor term in the conclusion when it is undistributed in its premise, and thus affirms universally in the conclusion what is affirmed partially in the premises.

Let us take an argument with an illicit process of the major term.

All M is P.
No M is S.
∴ No S is P.

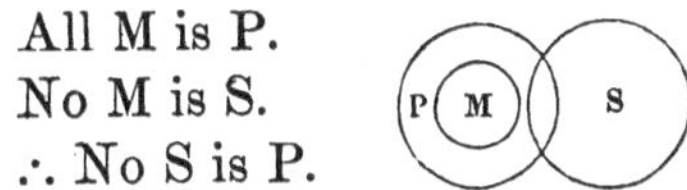

If the major premise is a case of coextension, the argument is valid, thus:

All M is P.
No M is S.
∴ No S is P.

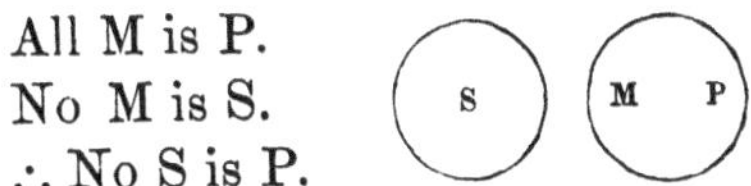

Let us now take an argument with an illicit process of the minor term.

All M is P.
All M is S.
∴ All S is P.

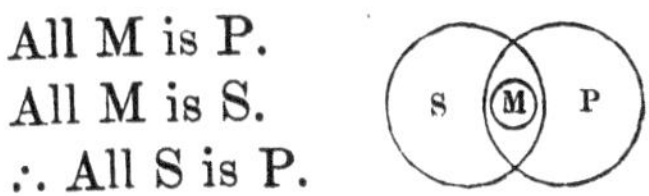

If the minor premise is a case of coextension, the argument is valid, thus:

All M is P.
All M is S.
∴ All S is P.

Let us take another argument with an illicit process of the minor term.

No M is P.
All M is S.
∴ No S is P.

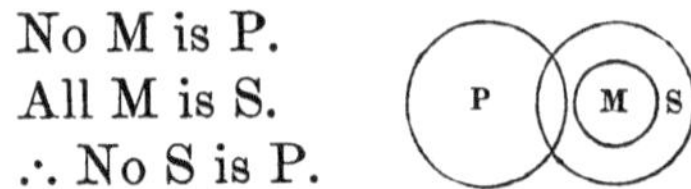

If the minor premise is a case of coextension, the argument is valid, thus:

No M is P.
All M is S.
∴ No S is P.

3. *Particular Premises.*

Except those cases in which an affirmative distributes the predicate, particular premises involve either an undistributed middle, or an illicit process, and, therefore, warrant no conclusion.

1*st.* Particular premises with an undistributed middle.

Some P is M.
Some S is M.
∴ Some S is P.

If the subject includes the predicate in either or both of the premises, the argument is valid, thus:

Some P is M.
Some S is M.
∴ Some S is P.

Again, take the following:

Some M is not P.
Some S is M.
∴ Some S is not P.

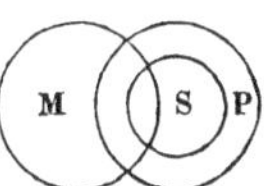

If the subject of the minor premise is coextensive with the predicate, the argument is valid, as in the following example:

Some M is not P.
Some S is M.
∴ Some S is not P.

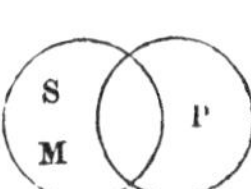

2*d*. Particular premises involving an illicit process of the major term.

Some M is P.
Some S is not M.
∴ Some S is not P.

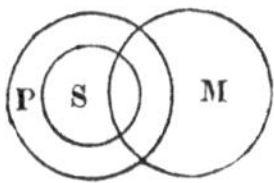

If the subject of the major premise includes the predicate, the argument is valid.

Some M is P.
Some S is not M.
∴ Some S is not P.

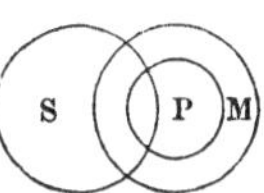

4. *Negative Premises.*

If both premises are negative, no conclusion is warranted; for the denial of certain relations between the middle term and the extremes, warrants neither the affirmation nor denial of any relation between the extremes:

No P is M.
No S is M.
∴ No S is P.

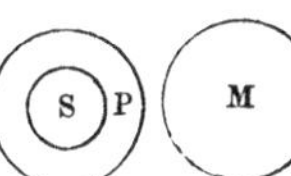

Take also the following:

Some M is not P.
No S is M.
∴ Some S is not P.

5. *An Affirmative Conclusion and One Negative Premise.*

The affirmative premise expresses the agreement, in whole or in part, of one of the extremes with the middle; and the negative premise, the disagreement of the other extreme with the middle; hence, the extremes must disagree with each other, or the conclusion is negative; hence, an affirmative conclusion would be unwarranted, as seen in the following examples:

No M is P.
All S is M.
∴ All S is P.

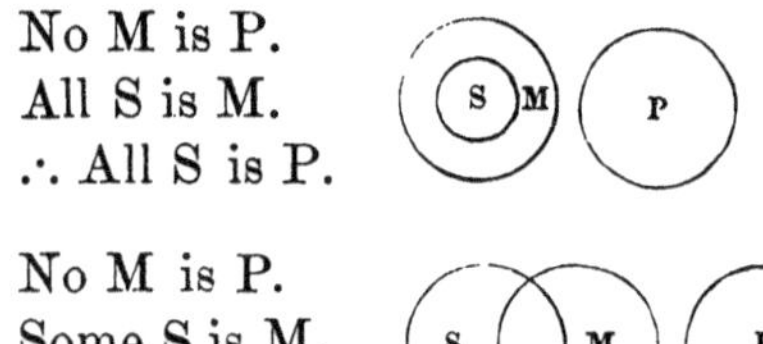

No M is P.
Some S is M.
∴ Some S is P.

6. *A Negative Conclusion from Affirmative Premises.*

Since the premises are affirmative, both extremes are affirmed to agree, in whole, or one in whole and the other in part with the middle; hence, they must agree with each other, or the conclusion is affirmative; hence, a negative conclusion would be unwarranted, as in the following examples:

All M is P.
All S is M.
∴ No S is P.

All M is P.
Some S is M.
∴ Some S is not P.

7. *A Universal Conclusion and a Particular Premise.*

This involves either an undistributed middle or illicit process:

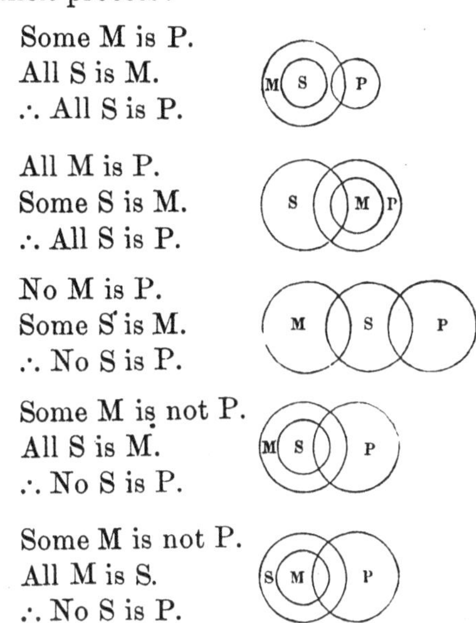

Some M is P.
All S is M.
∴ All S is P.

All M is P.
Some S is M.
∴ All S is P.

No M is P.
Some S is M.
∴ No S is P.

Some M is not P.
All S is M.
∴ No S is P.

Some M is not P.
All M is S.
∴ No S is P.

8. *Ambiguous Middle.*

Light is contrary to darkness.
Feathers are light.
∴ Feathers are contrary to darkness.

7. Rules.

1. If both premises are affirmative, the conclusion is affirmative.

2. If one premise is affirmative and the other negative, the conclusion is negative.

3. If both premises are negative, there is no conclusion.

4. If the conclusion is universal, both premises must be universal.

5. If both premises are particular, there is no conclusion except in case an affirmative distributes its predicate.

6. The middle term must not be ambiguous.

7. The middle term must be distributed in one of the premises.

8. No term must be distributed in the conclusion which is not distributed in one of the premises.

8. General Laws of the Syllogism.

1. Positive.
- *1st.* The truth of the premises involves the truth of the conclusion.
- *2d.* The falsity of the conclusion involves the falsity of one of the premises.

2. Negative.
- *1st.* The falsity of the premises does not involve the falsity of the conclusion.
- *2d.* The truth of the conclusion does not involve the truth of the premises.

9. Figure.

1. *Definition.*

Figure is the classification of syllogisms according to the position of the middle term with respect to the extremes in the premises.

Omitting the copula and the signs distinguishing the quantity and quality of the propositions, we have the following:

2. *Classification.*

Fig. 1.	M P. S M. S P.	In the first figure, the middle term is the subject of the major premise and predicate of the minor.
Fig. 2.	P M. S M. S P.	In the second figure, the middle term is the predicate of both premises.
Fig. 3.	M P. M S. S P.	In the third figure, the middle term is the subject of both premises.
Fig. 4.	P M. M S. S P.	In the fourth figure, the middle term is the predicate of the major premise and the subject of the minor.

For the opinions of Logicians concerning Fig. 4, see Mahan, pp. 121–4; Hamilton, pp. 285, 302, 626; Coppee, p. 117; Tappan, p. 347; Thompson, pp. 201–6; Wilson, p. 110; Whately, p. 96.

10. Mood.

1. *Definition.*

The mood of a syllogism is the arrangement of its propositions according to their quantity and quality.

2. *Remark.*

In the following discussion of the valid moods, we shall give those only which are universally valid, disregarding those exceptional cases, mentioned under the head of formal fallacies, which become valid in consequence of the distribution of the predicate of an affirmative.

3. *Positive Determination of the Valid Moods.*

1*st*. If the conclusion is (A) both premises must be (A). [Rules 1, 2, 4].

A A A is a valid mood, since { All M is P. All S is M. ∴ All S is P. } is a valid argument.

2*d*. If the conclusion is (E), one premise must be (A), the other (E). [R. 1, 2, 4].

AEE, EAE are valid moods, since { All P is M. No S is M. ∴ No S is P. } { No P is M. All S is M. ∴ No S is P. } are valid arguments.

3*d*. If the conclusion is (I), both premises must be affirmative, and one, at least, universal. [R. 1, 2, 5].

AAI, AII, IAI are valid moods, since { All M is P. All M is S. ∴ Some S is P. } { All M is P. Some M is S. ∴ Some S is P. } { Some M is P. All M is S. ∴ Some S is P. } are valid arguments.

4th. If the conclusion is (O), one premise must be affirmative, the other negative, and one, at least, universal. [R. 1, 2, 5].

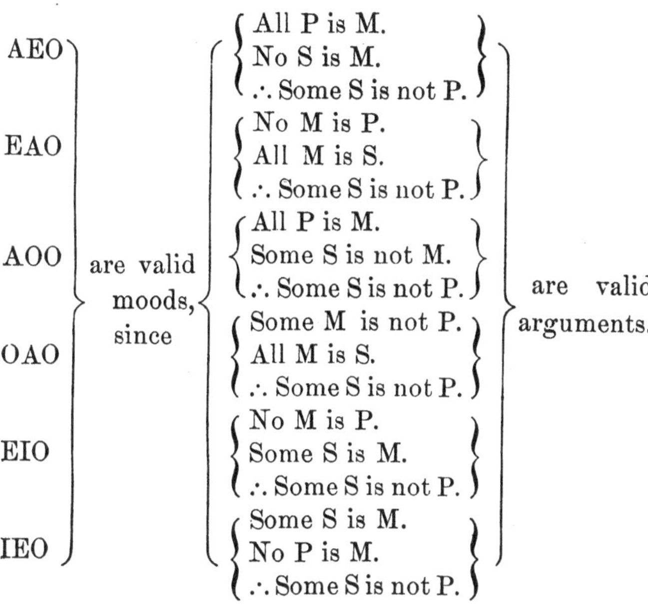

AEO, EAO, AOO, OAO, EIO, IEO are valid moods, since

All P is M.
No S is M.
∴ Some S is not P.

No M is P.
All M is S.
∴ Some S is not P.

All P is M.
Some S is not M.
∴ Some S is not P.

Some M is not P.
All M is S.
∴ Some S is not P.

No M is P.
Some S is M.
∴ Some S is not P.

Some S is M.
No P is M.
∴ Some S is not P.

are valid arguments.

4. *The Number of Valid Moods.*

One mood proves (A).
Two moods prove (E).
Three moods prove (I).
Six moods prove (O).

∴ $1+2+3+6=12$ = the number of valid moods.

The mood I E O is valid only on the condition that the minor premise stand first, otherwise there would be an illicit process of the major term.

5. *Negative Determination of the Valid Moods.*

Major Prem.	Minor Prem.	Con.	Moods.	Remarks.	Major Prem.	Minor Prem.	Con.	Moods.	Remarks.
A	A	A	A A A	Valid.	E	A	A	E A A	I. R. 2.
		E	A A E	Invalid R. 1.			E	E A E	V.
		I	A A I	V.			I	E A I	I. R. 2.
		O	A A O	I. R. 1.			O	E A O	V.
	E	A	A E A	I. R. 2.		E	A	E E A	I. R. 3.
		E	A E E	V.			E	E E E	I. R. 3.
		I	A E I	I. R. 2.			I	E E I	I. R. 3.
		O	A E O	V.			O	E E O	I. R. 3.
	I	A	A I A	I. R. 4.		I	A	E I A	I. R. 2. 4.
		E	A I E	I. R. 1. 4.			E	E I E	I. R. 4.
		I	A I I	V.			I	E I I	I. R. 2.
		O	A I O	I. R. 1.			O	E I O	V.
	O	A	A O A	I. R. 2. 4.		O	A	E O A	I. R. 3. 4.
		E	A O E	I. R. 4.			E	E O E	I. R. 3. 4.
		I	A O I	I. R. 2.			I	E O I	I. R. 3.
		O	A O O	V.			O	E O O	I. R. 3.

The valid moods are determined by first finding the invalid ones; that is, those violating one or more of the rules.

The remaining moods are, of course, valid.

Negative Determination Continued.

Major Prem.	Minor Prem.	Con.	Moods.	Remarks.	Major Prem.	Minor Prem.	Con.	Moods.	Remarks.
I	A	A	I A A	I. R. 4.	O	A	A	O A A	I. R. 2. 4.
		E	I A E	I. R. 1. 4.			E	O A E	I. R. 4.
		I	I A I	V.			I	O A I	I. R. 2.
		O	I A O	I. R. 1.			O	O A O	V.
	E	A	I E A	I. R. 2. 4.		E	A	O E A	I. R. 3. 4.
		E	I E E	I. R. 4.			E	O E E	I. R. 3. 4.
		I	I E I	I. R. 2.			I	O E I	I. R. 3.
		O	I E O	V.			O	O E O	I. R. 3.
	I	A	I I A	I. R. 4. 5.		I	A	O I A	I. R. 2. 4. 5.
		E	I I E	I. R. 1. 4. 5.			E	O I E	I. R. 4. 5.
		I	I I I	I. R. 5.			I	O I I	I. R. 2. 5.
		O	I I O	I. R. 1. 5.			O	O I O	I. R. 5.
	O	A	I O A	I. R. 2. 4. 5.		O	A	O O A	I. R. 3. 4. 5.
		E	I O E	I. R. 4. 5.			E	O O E	I. R. 3. 4. 5.
		I	I O I	I. R. 2. 5.			I	O O I	I. R. 3. 5.
		O	I O O	I. R. 5.			O	O O O	I. R. 3. 5.

The valid moods, as determined by the positive and negative methods, are the same.

In the columns headed "Remarks," R denotes rule; V, valid; I, invalid.

11. Figure I. $\left\{\begin{matrix}\text{M P.}\\ \text{S M.}\\ \text{S P.}\end{matrix}\right\}$

1. *Valid Moods in Figure I.*

To have an affirmative conclusion, both premises must be affirmative.

The major premise must be universal, otherwise the middle term would not be distributed, since it is not distributed as the predicate of the affirmative minor premise.

If the minor premise is universal, the conclusion may be universal or particular. If the minor premise is particular, the conclusion is particular.

$\therefore \left\{\begin{matrix}\text{A A A.}\\ \text{A A I.}\\ \text{A I I.}\end{matrix}\right\}$ are valid affirmative moods in Fig. 1.

To have a negative conclusion, the major premise must be negative in order to distribute the predicate which is distributed in the conclusion.

The minor premise must be affirmative, otherwise both premises would be negative, and there would be no conclusion.

The major premise must be universal, in order to distribute the middle term, since it is not distributed as the predicate of the affirmative minor premise.

If the minor premise is universal, the conclusion may be universal or particular.

If the minor premise is particular, the conclusion is particular.

$\therefore \left\{\begin{matrix}\text{E A E.}\\ \text{E A O.}\\ \text{E I O.}\end{matrix}\right\}$ are valid negative moods in Fig. 1.

Discarding A A I and E A O as involved in A A A and E A E, we have

2. *The Doctrine of Figure I.*

1*st*. The middle term is the subject of the major premise and predicate of the minor.

2*d*. The major premise is universal, and the minor, affirmative.

3*d*. The conclusion agrees in quality with the major premise, and in quantity with the minor.

4*th*. All forms of conclusion, (A), (E), (I), (O), are admissible in Figure 1.

3. *Aristotle's Dictum.*

Whatever is predicated, affirmatively or negatively, of any term distributed, may, in like manner, be predicated of whatever is contained under that term.

Let the dictum be applied to each of the following arguments.

4. *Arguments in Figure I with their Names.*

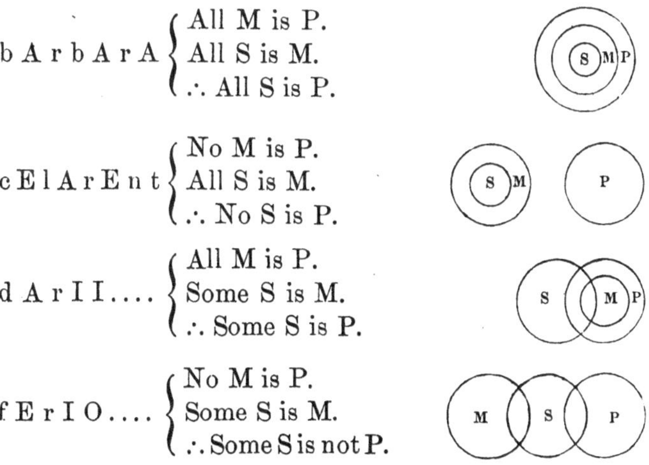

b A r b A r A { All M is P. All S is M. ∴ All S is P.

c E l A r E n t { No M is P. All S is M. ∴ No S is P.

d A r I I.... { All M is P. Some S is M. ∴ Some S is P.

f E r I O.... { No M is P. Some S is M. ∴ Some S is not P.

The vowels in these names designate the propositions.

12. Figure II. $\left\{\begin{array}{l} \text{P M.} \\ \text{S M.} \\ \text{S P.} \end{array}\right\}$

1. *Valid Moods in Figure II.*

In order to distribute the middle term, since it is the predicate of both premises, one of the premises must be negative; hence, the other premise must be affirmative, otherwise there would be no conclusion.

Since one premise is affirmative and the other negative, the conclusion is negative, and, therefore, its predicate is distributed; hence, the major premise must be universal in order to distribute its subject, which is the predicate of the conclusion.

If the minor premise is universal, the conclusion may be universal or particular.

If the minor premise is particular, the conclusion is particular.

$$\therefore \left\{\begin{array}{l} \left.\begin{array}{l}\text{EAE}\\ \text{AEE}\end{array}\right\} \text{give universal negative conclusions,} \\ \left.\begin{array}{l}\text{EAO}\\ \text{AEO}\\ \text{EIO}\\ \text{AOO}\end{array}\right\} \text{give particular negative conclusions,}\end{array}\right\} \text{and are valid moods in Fig. 2.}$$

Discarding the moods E A O and A E O as involved in E A E and A E E, we have, from the four remaining moods,

2. *The Doctrine of Figure II.*

1*st.* The middle term is the predicate of both premises.

2*d.* One premise is affirmative and the other negative.

3*d.* The major premise is universal.

4*th.* The conclusion is negative and agrees in quantity with the minor premise.

3. *Arguments in Figure II with their Names.*

c E s A r E... { No P is M. / All S is M. / ∴ No S is P.

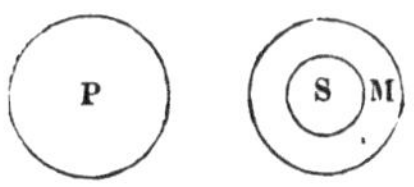

P S M

c A m E s t r E s { All P is M. / No S is M. / ∴ No S is P.

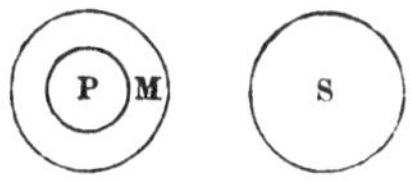

P M S

f E s t I n O.. { No P is M. / Some S is M. / ∴ Some S is not P.

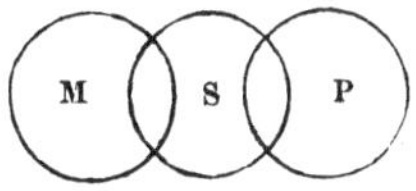

M S P

f A k O r O... { All P is M. / Some S is not M. / ∴ Some S is not P.

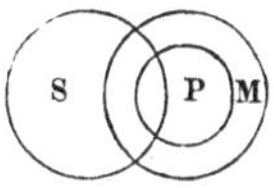

S P M

Aristotle's dictum, given on page sixty-five, does not apply directly to any of the four figures except the first.

13. Figure III. $\left\{\begin{matrix} M & P. \\ M & S. \\ S & P. \end{matrix}\right\}$

1. *Valid Moods in Figure III.*

In order to distribute the middle term, one of the premises must be universal.

If both premises be universal affirmative, and a universal affirmative conclusion be drawn, there would be an illicit process of the minor term.

If both premises be universal, the major negative and the minor affirmative, and a universal negative conclusion be drawn, there would be an illicit process of the minor term.

If both premises be universal, the major affirmative and the minor negative, and a universal negative conclusion be drawn, there would be an illicit process of the major term.

Hence, in Fig. 3, the conclusion must be particular.

If the conclusion is affirmative, both premises must be affirmative.

If the conclusion is negative, the major term is distributed; hence, the major premise must be negative, and, therefore, the minor premise, affirmative.

<table>
<tr><td rowspan="6">∴</td><td>AAI
IAI
AII</td><td>give particular affirmative conclusions,</td><td rowspan="2">and are valid moods in Fig. 3.</td></tr>
<tr><td>EAO
OAO
EIO</td><td>give particular negative conclusions,</td></tr>
</table>

2. *The Doctrine of Figure III.*

1*st.* The middle term is the subject of both premises.

2*d.* One premise is universal and the minor affirmative.

3*d.* The conclusion is particular and agrees in quality with the major premise.

3. *Arguments in Figure III with their Names.*

d A r A p t I. { All M is P. / All M is S. / ∴ Some S is P.

d I s A m I s. { Some M is P. / All M is S. / ∴ Some S is P.

d A t I s I... { All M is P. / Some M is S. / ∴ Some S is P.

f E l A p t O n { No M is P. / All M is S. / ∴ Some S is not P.

d O k A m O { Some M is not P. / All M is S. / ∴ Some S is not P.

f E r I s O... { No M is P. / Some M is S. / ∴ Some S is not P.

14. Figure IV. $\left\{\begin{matrix} P\ M. \\ M\ S. \\ S\ P. \end{matrix}\right\}$

1. *Valid Moods in Figure IV.*

In order to distribute the middle term, the major premise must be negative or the minor, universal.

If the conclusion is affirmative, both premises must be affirmative, and the minor premise universal in order to distribute the middle term which is not distributed as the predicate of the affirmative major premise.

The affirmative conclusion must be particular, otherwise there would be an illicit process of the minor term.

If the conclusion is a universal negative, both premises must be universal, the minor, negative, in order to distribute its predicate which is distributed as the subject of the universal conclusion, and, therefore, the major premise must be affirmative.

If the conclusion is a particular negative, the major premise must be universal in order to distribute its subject which is distributed as the predicate of the negative conclusion; and if the major premise is affirmative, its predicate, which is the middle term, is undistributed; hence, the minor premise must, in this case, be a universal negative; but if the major premise is negative, the minor premise may be either a universal or a particular affirmative.

∴ AAI, IAI give affirmative conclusions, AEE, AEO, EAO, EIO give negative conclusions, and are valid moods in Figure 4.

Discarding A E O as involved in A E E, we have

2. *The Doctrine of Figure IV.*

1st. The middle term is the predicate of the major premise and subject of the minor.

2d. Either the major premise must be negative or the minor, universal.

3d. If the conclusion is affirmative, both premises must be affirmative; the minor, universal, the major, universal or particular, and the conclusion particular.

4th. If the conclusion is a universal negative, the premises must both be universal; the minor, negative, the major, affirmative.

5th. If the conclusion is a particular negative, the major premise must be a universal negative, and the minor premise may be either a universal or a particular affirmative.

3. *Arguments in Figure IV with their Names.*

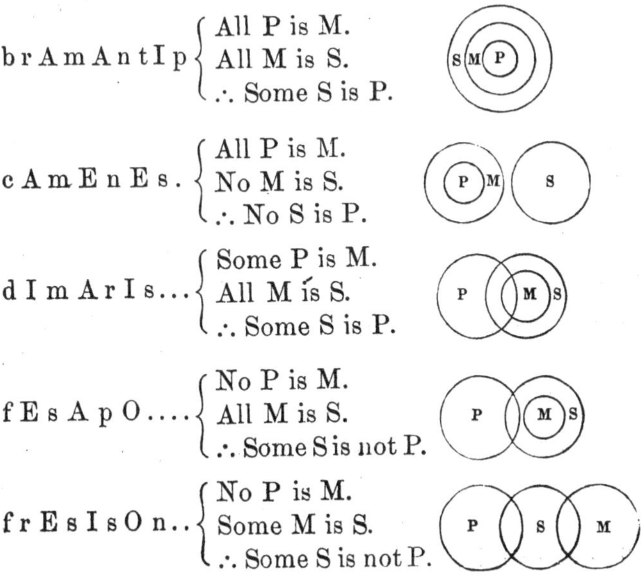

brAmAntIp: All P is M. All M is S. ∴ Some S is P.

cAmEnEs: All P is M. No M is S. ∴ No S is P.

dImArIs: Some P is M. All M is S. ∴ Some S is P.

fEsApO: No P is M. All M is S. ∴ Some S is not P.

frEsIsOn: No P is M. Some M is S. ∴ Some S is not P.

15. Summary of the Names of the Arguments.

Fig. I. b A r b A r A, c E l A r E n t, d A r I I, f E r I O.

Fig. II. c E s A r E, c A m E s t r E s, f E s t I n O, f A k O r O.

Fig. III. d A r A p t I, d I s A m I s, d A t I s I, f E l A p t O n, d O k A m O, f E r I s O.

Fig. IV. b r A m A n t I p, c A m E n E s, d I m-A r I s, f E s A p O, f r E s I s O n.

16. Signification of the Consonants in Fig's II, III, IV.

1. *Consonants denoting Results.*

1*st.* Initial *b* denotes reduction to b A r b A r A.
2*d.* Initial *c* denotes reduction to c E l A r E n t.
3*d.* Initial *d* denotes reduction to d A r I I.
4*th.* Initial *f* denotes reduction to f E r I O.

2. *Consonants denoting Transformation.*

1*st.* *m* denotes that the premises are to be transposed.

2*d.* *s* denotes that the proposition represented by the preceding vowel is to be converted simply.

3*d.* *p* denotes that the proposition represented by the preceding vowel is to be converted by limitation; but *p* in b r A m A n t I p denotes that when the reduction is made, a universal conclusion is warranted.

4*th.* *k* denotes that the preceding *A* is to be changed into *E*, and the result converted simply, and that the preceding *O* is to be changed into *I*, and the result converted simply.

17. Direct Reduction.

1. *Object.*

The object of reduction is to bring arguments in Figures II, III, and IV to the test of Aristotle's Dictum, which is applicable only to arguments in Figure I.

2. *Fig. II to Fig. I.*

cEsArE	No P is M. All S is M. ∴ No S is P.	=	cElArEnt	No M is P. All S is M. ∴ No S is P.
cAmEstrEs	All P is M. No S is M. ∴ Nŏ S is P.	=	cElArEnt	No M is S. All P is M. ∴ No P is S.
fEstInO	No P is M. Some S is M. ∴ Some S is not P.	=	fErIO	No M is P. Some S is M. ∴ Some S is not P.
fAkOrO	All P is M. Some S is not M. ∴ Some S is not P.	=	fErIO	No non-M is P. Seme S is non-M. ∴ Some S is not P.

3. *Fig. III to Fig. I.*

dArAptI	All M is P. All M is S. ∴ Some S is P.	=	dArII	All M is P. Some S is M. ∴ Some S is P.
dIsAmIs	Some M is P. All M is S. ∴ Some S is P.	=	dArII	All M is S. Some P is M. ∴ Some P is S.
dAtIsI	All M is P. Some M is S. ∴ Some S is P.	=	dArII	All M is P. Some S is M. ∴ Some S is P.
fElAptOn	No M is P. All M is S. ∴ Some S is not P.	=	fErIO	No M is P. Some S is M. ∴ Some S is not P

dOkAmO	Some M is not P. All M is S. ∴ Some S is not P.	= dArII	All M is S. Some non-P is M. ∴ Some non-P is S.
fErIsO	No M is P. Some M is S. ∴ Some S is not P.	= fErIO	No M is P. Some S is M. ∴ Some S is not P.

4. *Fig. IV to Fig. I.*

brAmAntIp	All P is M. All M is S. ∴ Some S is P.	= bArbArA	All M is S. All P is M. ∴ All P is S.
cAmEnEs	All P is M. No M is S. ∴ No S is P.	= cElArEnt	No M is S. All P is M. ∴ No P is S.
dImArIs	Some P is M. All M is S. ∴ Some S is P.	= dArII	All M is S. Some P is M. ∴ Some P is S.
fEsApO	No P is M. All M is S. ∴ Some S is not P.	= fErIO	No M is P. Some S is M. ∴ Some S is not P.
frEsIsOn	No P is M. Some M is S. ∴ Some S is not P.	= fErIO	No M is P. Some S is M. ∴ Some S is not P.

18. Indirect Reduction.

1. *Notation.*

t = true, f = false, c = contradictory, c' = contrary, h = hypothesis.

2. *Fig. II to Fig. I.*

Rule.

Substitute the contradictory of the conclusion for the minor premise.

cEsArE′	No P is M. All S is M. ∴ No S is P.	gives fErIO	No P is M. Some S is P. ∴ Some S is not M

But O is the *c* of A which is *t* by *h*; ∴ O is *f*; ∴ either E or I must be *f*; but E is *t* by *h*; ∴ I is *f*; but I is the *c* of E′; ∴ E′ is *t*.

cAmEstrE′s	All P is M. No S is M. ∴ No S is P.	gives dArII′	All P is M. Some S is P. ∴ Some S is M.

But I′ is the *c* of E which is *t* by *h*; ∴ I′ is *f*; ∴ either A or I must be *f*; but A is *t* by *h*; ∴ I is *f*; but I is the *c* of E′; ∴ E′ is *t*.

fEstInO	No P is M. Some S is M. ∴ Some S is not P.	gives cElArE′nt	No P is M. All S is P. ∴ No S is M.

But E′ is the *c* of I which is *t* by *h*; ∴ E′ is *f*; ∴ either E or A must be *f*; but E is *t* by *h*; ∴ A is *f*; but A is the *c* of O; ∴ O is *t*.

fAkOrO′	All P is M. Some S is not M. ∴ Some S is not P.	gives bArbA′rA″	All P is M. All S is P. ∴ All S is M.

But A″ is the *c* of O which is *t* by *h*; ∴ A″ is *f*; ∴ either A or A′ must be *f*; but A is *t* by *h*; ∴ A′ is *f*; but A′ is the *c* of O′; ∴ O′ is *t*.

3. *Fig. III to Fig. I.*

Rule.

Substitute the contradictory of the conclusion for the major premise.

dArA′ptI	All M is P. All M is S. ∴ Some S is P.	gives cElA′rE′nt	No S is P. All M is S. ∴ No M is P.

But E′ is the *c′* of A which is *t* by *h*; ∴ E′ is *f*; ∴ either E or A′ must be *f*; but A′ is *t* by *h*; ∴ E is *f*; but E is the *c* of I; ∴ I is *t*.

d I s A m I′ s	Some M is P. All M is S. ∴ Some S is P.	gives	c E l A r E′ n t	No S is P. All M is S. ∴ No M is P.

But E′ is the *c* of I which is *t* by *h*; ∴ E′ is *f*; ∴ either E or A must be *f*; but A is *t* by *h*; ∴ E is *f*; but E is the *c* of I′; ∴ I′ is *t*.

d A t I s I′	All M is P. Some M is S. ∴ Some S is P.	gives	f E r I O	No S is P. Some M is S. ∴ Some M is not P.

But O is the *c* of A which is *t* by *h*; ∴ O is *f*; ∴ either E or I must be *f*; but I is *t* by *h*; ∴ E is *f*; but E is the *c* of I′; ∴ I′ is *t*.

f E l A p t O n	No M is P. All M is S. ∴ Some S is not P.	gives	b A′ r b A r A″	All S is P. All M is S. ∴ All M is P.

But A″ is the *c*′ of E which is *t* by *h*; ∴ A″ is *f*; ∴ either A′ or A must be *f*; but A is *t* by *h*; ∴ A′ is *f*; but A′ is *c* of O; ∴ O is *t*.

d O k A m O′	Some M is not P. All M is S. ∴ Some S is not P.	gives	b A′ r b A r A″	All S is P. All M is S. ∴ All M is P.

But A″ is the *c* of O which is *t* by *h*; ∴ A″ is *f*; ∴ either A′ or A must be *f*; but A is *t* by *h*; ∴ A′ is *f*· but A′ is the *c* of O′; ∴ O′ is *t*.

f E r I s O	No M is P. Some M is S. ∴ Some S is not P.	gives	d A r I I′	All S is P. Some M is S. ∴ Some M is P.

But I′ is the *c* of E which is *t* by *h*; ∴ I′ is *f*; ∴ either A or I must be *f*; but I is *t* by *h*; ∴ A is *f*; but A is the *c* of O; ∴ O is *t*.

4. *Fig. IV to Fig. I.*

Rule.

Substitute the contradictory of the conclusion for the major premise, but in c A m E n E s for the minor.

brAmA′ntIp	All P is M. All M is S. ∴ Some S is P.	gives c E l A′ r E′ n t	No S is P. All M is S. ∴ No M is P.

But the converse of E′ is the *c′* of A which is *t* by *h*; ∴ E′ is *f*; ∴ either E or A′ must be *f*; but A′ is *t* by *h*; ∴ E is *f*; but E is the *c* of I; ∴ I is *t*.

c A m E n E′ s	All P is M. No M is S. ∴ No S is P.	gives d A r I I′	All P is M. Some S is P. ∴ Some S is M.

But the converse of I′ is the *c* of E which is *t* by *h*; ∴ I′ is *f*; ∴ either A or I must be *f*; but A is *t* by *h*; ∴ I is *f*; but I is the *c* of E′; ∴ E′ is *t*.

d I m A r I′ s	Some P is M. All M is S. ∴ Some S is P.	gives c E l A r E′ n t	No S is P. All M is S. ∴ No M is P.

But the converse of E′ is the *c* of I which is *t* by *h*; ∴ E′ is *f*; ∴ either E or A must be *f*; but A is *t* by *h*; ∴ E is *f*; but E is the *c* of I′; ∴ I′ is *t*.

f E s A p O	No P is M. All M is S. ∴ Some S is not P.	gives b A′ r b A r A″	All S is P. All M is S. ∴ All M is P.

But the converse of A″ is the *c* of E which is *t* by *h*; ∴ A″ is *f*; ∴ either A′ or A must be *f*; but A is *t* by *h*; ∴ A′ is *f*; but A′ is the *c* of O; ∴ O is *t*.

f r E s I s O n { No P is M. / Some M is S. / ∴ Some S is not P. } gives d A r I I′ { All S is P. / Some M is S. / ∴ Some M is P. }

But the converse of I′ is the *c* of E which is *t* by *h*, ∴ I′ is *f*; ∴ either A or I must be *f*; but I is *t* by *h*; ∴ A is *f*; but A is the *c* of O; ∴ O is *t*.

19. Examples.

Give the figure, mood, and name of the following arguments, and those in the II, III, or IV Figure, reduce to the I, both by direct and indirect reduction.

1. Every event has a cause.
   The world is an event.
   ∴ The world has a cause.

2. No vicious conduct is praiseworthy.
   All heroic conduct is praiseworthy.
   ∴ No heroic conduct is vicious.

3. All diligent scholars deserve reward.
   Some boys are diligent scholars.
   ∴ Some boys deserve reward.

4. All good reasoners are candid.
   Some infidels are not candid.
   ∴ Some infidels are not good reasoners.

5. All oaks are trees.
   All trees are vegetables.
   ∴ Some vegetables are oaks.

6. Every wicked man is discontented.
   No happy man is discontented.
   ∴ No happy man is a wicked man.

7. All wits are dreaded.
   All wits are admired.
   ∴ Some who are admired are dreaded.

8. Some slaves are not discontented.
All slaves are wronged.
∴ Some who are wronged are not discontented.

9. No immoral acts are proper amusements.
All proper amusements give pleasure.
∴ Some things that give pleasure are not immoral acts.

10. All expedient things are conformable to nature.
Nothing conformable to nature is hurtful to society.
∴ Nothing hurtful to society is expedient.

11. No one governed by passion is free.
All sensualists are governed by passion.
∴ No sensualist is free.

12. No just act will result in evil.
Some association will result in evil.
∴ Some association is not a just act.

13. No impediment to commerce is favorable to national prosperity.
Some taxes are impediments to commerce.
∴ Some taxes are not favorable to national prosperity.

14. No Science is capable of perfection.
All Science is worthy of culture.
∴ Something worthy of culture is not capable of perfection.

15. All pride is inconsistent with religion.
Some pride is commended by the world.
∴ Something commended by the world is inconsistent with religion.

16. Some noble characters are not philosophers.
All noble characters are worthy of admiration.
∴ Some worthy of admiration are not philosophers.

17. No prejudices are compatible with perfection,
Some prejudices are innocent.
∴ Some innocent things are not compatible with perfection.

18. Some taxes are oppressive measures.
All oppressive measures should be repealed.
∴ Some things which should be repealed are taxes.

19. No fallacious argument is a legitimate mode of persuasion.
Some legitimate modes of persuasion fail to gain acquiescence.
∴ Some arguments which fail to gain acquiescence are not fallacious.

20. Hypothetical Syllogisms.

1. *Definition.*

An hypothetical syllogism is an argument whose form is determined by the Law of Reason and Consequent.

2. *Examples.*

1*st.* Constructive.
If A has the fever, he is sick.
But A has the fever.
∴ A is sick.

2*d.* Destructive.
If A has the fever, he is sick.
But A is not sick.
∴ A has not the fever.

3. *The Propositions of an Hypothetical Syllogism.*

1*st.* The major premise is an hypothetical proposition, definite and affirmative, enouncing the dependency between a conditioning antecedent and a condiioned consequent, but affirming nothing in regard to the actual existence of either.

2*d.* The minor premise is a categorical proposition either affirming the conditioning antecedent or denying the conditioned consequent.

3*d.* The conclusion is a categorical proposition affirming the consequent, if the antecedent is affirmed in the minor premise; or denying the antecedent, if the consequent is denied in the minor premise.

4. *Laws.*

1*st.* Positive.
- *a.* Affirming the antecedent affirms the consequent.
- *b.* Denying the consequent denies the antecedent.

2*d.* Negative.
- *a.* Denying the antecedent does not deny the consequent.
- *b.* Affirming the consequent does not affirm the antecedent.

If the predicate of the antecedent is co-exténsive with the predicate of the consequent, the negative laws become positive.

5. *Categorical and Hypothetical Syllogisms Compared.*

Though it be true that an hypothetical syllogism has an hypothetical proposition for its major premise, yet it does not follow that every syllogism which has an hypothetical major premise is an hypothetical syllogism. Thus, take the following:

If the Scriptures came from God, they are entitled to our faith.

If they are not an imposture, they came from God.

If, therefore, they are not an imposture, they are entitled to our faith.

6. *Reduction of Hypothetical Syllogisms to Categorical.*

1*st*. If the major premise contains three terms, one being a middle, thus:

If A is B, A is C. But A is B. ∴ A is C.	=	B is C. A is B. ∴ A is C.

2*d*. If the major premise contains four terms, thus:

If A is B, C is D. But A is B. ∴ C is D.	=	B is D. A is B. ∴ A is D. A is D. C is A. ∴ C is D.

21. Disjunctive Syllogisms.

1. *Definition.*

A disjunctive syllogism is an argument whose form is determined by the Law of Contradictories.

2. *Examples.*

1*st*. Affirmative.	Plato is either learned or unlearned. But Plato is learned. ∴ Plato is not unlearned.
2*d*. Negative.	The patient will live or die. He will not live. ∴ He will die.

3. *The Propositions of a Disjunctive Syllogism.*

1*st*. The major premise is a disjunctive proposition, universal and affirmative, having the opposition, *a*. Contrary, as S is either P or Q, determined *a posteriori*, and thus brought under the Law of Contradictories.

b. Contradictory.
- *α*. In the copula, as S either is or is not P.
- *β*. In the terms, as S is either P or non-P.

2*d*. The minor premise is a categorical proposition, universal or particular, affirmative or negative, removing the disjunction.

3*d*. The conclusion is a categorical proposition, agreeing in quantity, but disagreeing in quality, with the minor premise.

4. *Disjunctive Syllogisms having two Disjunctive Members.*

1*st*. Affirmative.
- S is either P or Q.
- But S is P.
- ∴ S is not Q.

2*d*. Negative.
- S is either P or Q.
- But S is not Q.
- ∴ S is P.

5. *Laws.*

1*st*. Affirming either alternative denies the other.

2*d*. Denying either alternative affirms the other.

6. *Disjunctive Syllogisms having more than two Disjunctive Members.*

1*st*. Affirmative.
- *a*.
  - A is either B, C, D, or E.
  - But A is B.
  - ∴ A is neither C, D, nor E.
- *b*.
  - A is either B, C, D, or E.
  - But A is either B or C.
  - ∴ A is neither D nor E.

2*d*. Negative.

a.
A is either B, C, D, or E.
But A is neither B, C, nor D.
∴ A is E.

b.
A is either B, C, D, or E.
But A is neither B nor C.
∴ A is either D or E.

7. *Laws.*

1*st.* Affirming a part of the disjunctives, determinately or indeterminately, in the minor premise, denies all the others in the conclusion.

2*d.* Denying a part of the disjunctives in the minor premise, affirms the rest, in the conclusion, determinately or indeterminately, according as one or more remain.

8. *Categorical and Disjunctive Syllogisms Compared.*

Though it be true that a disjunctive syllogism has a disjunctive major premise, it does not follow that every syllogism with a disjunctive major premise is a disjunctive syllogism.

Take the following:

B is either C or D.
A is B.
∴ A is either C or D.

This syllogism is not disjunctive, but categorical, since its form is determined, not by the Law of Contradictories, but by the Law of Identity.

22. Dilemmatic Syllogisms.

1. *Definition.*

A dilemmatic syllogism is a syllogism having a hypothetical major premise and a disjunctive minor.

2. *Forms.*

$$\textit{1st.}\ \left\{\begin{array}{l}\text{If A is B, X is Y.}\\ \text{If C is D, X is Y.}\\ \text{If E is F, X is Y.}\end{array}\right.$$

$$\text{But}\ \left\{\begin{array}{l} \textit{a.}\ \text{Either}\ \left\{\begin{array}{l}\text{A is B, or}\\ \text{C is D, or}\\ \text{E is F.}\end{array}\right\} \therefore \text{X is Y.}\\ \textit{b.}\ \text{X is not Y.}\ \therefore \text{Neither}\ \left\{\begin{array}{l}\text{A is B, nor}\\ \text{C is D, nor}\\ \text{E is F.}\end{array}\right.\end{array}\right.$$

$$\textit{2d.}\ \left\{\begin{array}{l}\text{If A is B, C is D.}\\ \text{If A is B, E is F.}\\ \text{If A is B, G is H.}\end{array}\right.$$

$$\text{But}\ \left\{\begin{array}{l} \textit{a.}\ \text{A is B.}\ \therefore \left\{\begin{array}{l}\text{C is D, and}\\ \text{E is F, and}\\ \text{G is H.}\end{array}\right.\\ \textit{b.}\ \text{Either}\ \left\{\begin{array}{l}\text{C is not D, or}\\ \text{E is not F, or}\\ \text{G is not H.}\end{array}\right\} \therefore \text{A is not B.}\end{array}\right.$$

$$\textit{3d.}\ \left\{\begin{array}{l}\text{If A is B, G is H.}\\ \text{If C is D, I is K.}\\ \text{If E is F, L is M.}\end{array}\right.$$

$$\text{But}\ \left\{\begin{array}{l} \textit{a.}\ \text{Either}\left\{\begin{array}{l}\text{A is B, or}\\ \text{C is D, or}\\ \text{E is F.}\end{array}\right\} \therefore \text{Either}\left\{\begin{array}{l}\text{G is H, or}\\ \text{I is K, or}\\ \text{L is M.}\end{array}\right.\\ \textit{b.}\ \text{Either}\left\{\begin{array}{l}\text{G is not H, or}\\ \text{I is not K, or}\\ \text{L is not M.}\end{array}\right\} \therefore \text{Either}\left\{\begin{array}{l}\text{A is not B, or}\\ \text{C is not D, or}\\ \text{E is not F.}\end{array}\right.\end{array}\right.$$

3. *Remark.*

The forms, *1st.*, *b.*, and *2d.*, *a.*, are not, strictly, dilemmatic syllogisms, since the minor premise is not disjunctive.

23. Enthymemes.

1. *Definition.*

An enthymeme is a syllogism with one proposition suppressed.

It differs from the ordinary syllogism, not in thought, but in enouncement.

2. *Etymology.*

The word enthymeme is from ἐνθύμημα, ἐν and θυμός, in the mind.

3. *Examples of Enthymemes.*

1*st.*	With a suppressed major premise.	Cæsar is a man. ∴ Cæsar is mortal.
2*d.*	With a suppressed minor premise.	All men are mortal. ∴ Cæsar is mortal.
3*d.*	With a suppressed conclusion.	All men are mortal. Cæsar is a man.

Each of these enthymemes is equivalent to

The complete syllogism.	All men are mortal. Cæsar is a man. ∴ Cæsar is mortal.

24. Prosyllogism and Episyllogism.

1. *Definitions.*

1*st.* A prosyllogism is an argument whose conclusion is one of the premises of another argument.

2*d*. An episyllogism is an argument one of whose premises is the conclusion of another argument.

2. *Example.*

Prosyllogism. { All B is C. / All A is B. / ∴ All A is C.

Main Syllogism. { All C is D. / All A is C. / ∴ All A is D.

Episyllogism. { All D is E. / All A is D. / ∴ All A is E.

25. Sorites.

1. *Definition.*

The Sorites or Chain Syllogism is a compound argument.

2. *Forms.*

1*st*. When the predicate of each premise is the subject of the next.

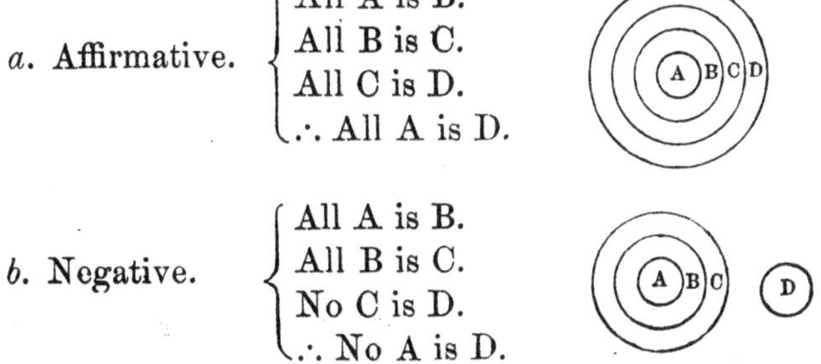

a. Affirmative. { All A is B. / All B is C. / All C is D. / ∴ All A is D.

b. Negative. { All A is B. / All B is C. / No C is D. / ∴ No A is D.

2*d*. When the subject of each premise is the predicate of the next.

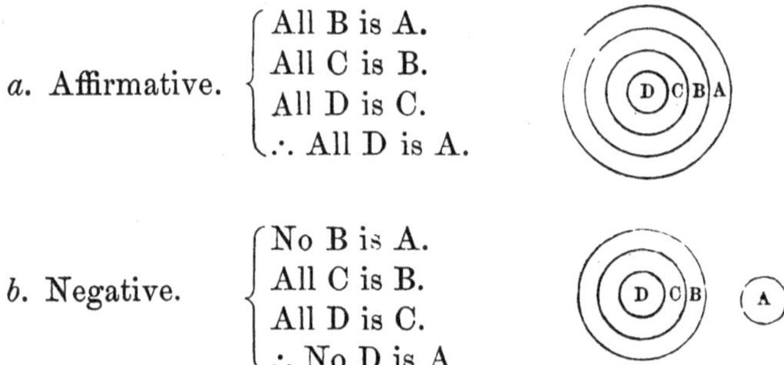

a. Affirmative.

All B is A.
All C is B.
All D is C.
∴ All D is A.

b. Negative.

No B is A.
All C is B.
All D is C.
∴ No D is A.

3*d*. When the first and second forms are combined.

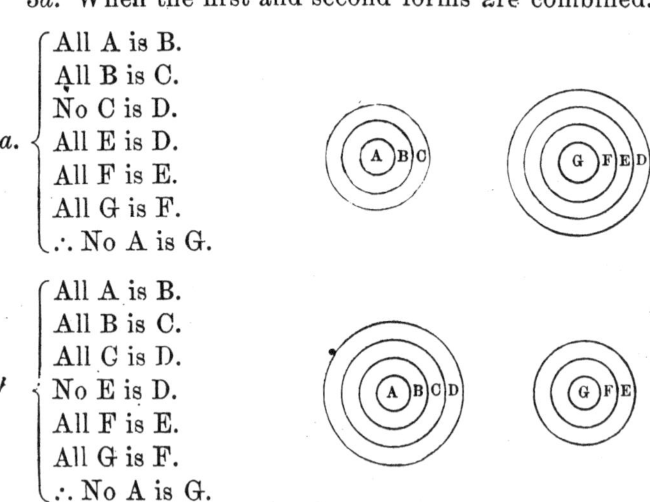

a.

All A is B.
All B is C.
No C is D.
All E is D.
All F is E.
All G is F.
∴ No A is G.

b.

All A is B.
All B is C.
All C is D.
No E is D.
All F is E.
All G is F.
∴ No A is G.

3. *Laws.*

1*st*. The first premise in the first form, the last in the second, and the first or last in the third are the only ones that can be particular; and the subject of the particular premise will be the subject of the conclusion.

2*d*. Only one premise can be negative—the last in the first form and the first in the second form.

3*d*. In the third form, one premise must be negative—the last in the first series, or the first in the second series.

4. *Expansion of the Sorites.*

1*st*.		=	
	All A is B. All B is C. All C is D. ∴ All A is D.	=	All A is B. All B is C. ∴ All A is C. All C is D. All A is C. ∴ All A is D.

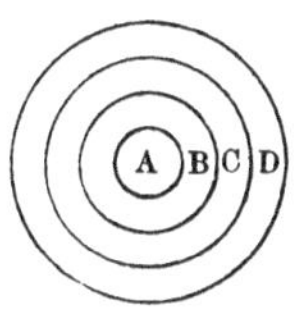

A B C D

2*d*. Expand
- The mind is a thinking substance.
- A thinking substance is a spirit.
- A spirit has no composition of parts.
- That which has no composition of parts is indissoluble.
- That which is indissoluble is immortal.
- ∴ The mind is immortal.

26. The Epichirema.

1. *Definition.*

The Epichirema is an argument in which the reasons for the premises are stated in connection with them.

2. *Etymology.*

The word *epichirema* is derived from ἐπιχείρημα, from ἐπί and χείρ, and literally signifies to lay hands upon.

3. *Examples.*

1*st*.
- A is B, for A is C and C is B.
- D is A, for D is E and E is A.
- ∴ D is B.

L. 8

2*d.*
- All true patriots are friends to religion, because religion is the basis of national prosperity.
- Some great statesmen are not friends to religion, because their lives are not in accordance with its precepts.
- ∴ Some great statesmen are not true patriots.

27. The Unfigured Syllogism.

1. *Definition.*

The Unfigured Syllogism is an argument in which the terms of the propositions do not sustain to each other the relation of subject and predicate.

2. *Examples.*

1*st.* Positive.
- A and B always coexist.
- B and C always coexist.
- ∴ A and C always coexist.

2*d.* Negative.
- A and B always coexist.
- B and C never coexist.
- ∴ A and C never coexist.

3. *Laws.*

1*st.* As far as two terms agree with a third, so far they agree with each other.

2*d.* As far as one term agrees and another disagrees with a third, so far they disagree with each other.

28. The Reductio ad Absurdum.

1. *Definitions.*

1*st.* An axiom is a self-evident truth.

2*d.* An absurdity is a self-evident falsity.

For every axiom there is a corresponding absurdity, and for every absurdity there is a corresponding axiom, and the two are contradictories.

3*d.* The *reductio ad absurdum* is an argument in which a proposition is proved true by showing that the supposition that it is false, or, which is the same thing, that its contradictory is true, involves an absurdity.

2. *Principles.*

1*st.* All truths harmonize.

2*d.* If the premises of an argument are true, and the reasoning logical, the conclusion is true.

3*d.* If the conclusion of an argument is false, and one of the premises true, and the reasoning logical, the other premise is false.

4*th* If a proposition is true, its contradictory is false, and if a proposition is false, its contradictory is true.

3. *Application.*

To prove a given proposition true by the *reductio ad absurdum* method, we assume it false; that is, we assume its contradictory true.

We then combine this assumed proposition, with a proposition known to be true, in a logical argument which gives a false conclusion, false either because it is the contradictory of an axiom, and hence absurd, or because it is the contradictory of an established proposition, hence involving the absurdity that one truth contradicts another.

Since the conclusion is false, and one of the premises true, and the reasoning logical, the other premise which is the assumed proposition, the contradictory of the given proposition, is false; and if false, its contradictory, or the given proposition is true, and is, hence. demonstrated.

4. *Example.*

Let it be required to prove the following proposition:

If a straight line meet two other straight lines at a common point, making the sum of the two contiguous angles equal to two right angles, the two lines which are met will form one and the same straight line.

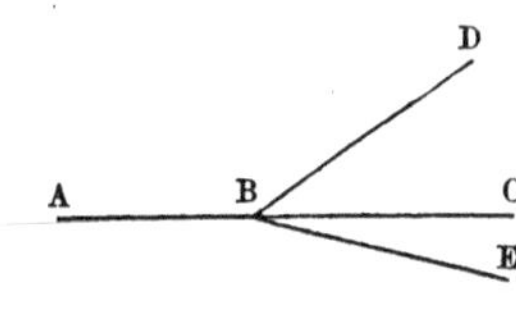

Let D B meet A B and C B at their common point B, making A B D + D B C = two right angles, then will A B and B C form one and the same right line.

For, if not, suppose A B and any other line than B C, as B E, to form the same straight line.

Then will A B D + D B E = two right angles.

But, by hypothesis, A B D + D B C = two right angles.

Hence, A B D + D B C = A B D + D B E.

Subtracting A B D from each of these equals, we have D B C = D B E.

That is, a part is equal to the whole, which is absurd.

Hence, the supposition that A B and B C do not form one and the same straight line, or, which is the same, that A B and some other line than B C, as B E, form one and the same straight line, involves the absurdity that a part is equal to the whole; and, therefore, this supposition is false.

But if it is false that A B and B C do not form one and the same straight line, it is true that A B and B C do form one and the same straight line.

29. The Exhaustive Method.

1. *Definition.*

The exhaustive method of demonstration is the method of proving that a certain relation exists between two terms by considering all possible relations, one of which must be true, and by showing that all except one is false, because involving absurdities, and, hence, that the remaining case must be true.

2. *Compared with the Reductio ad Absurdum.*

In the *reductio ad absurdum* method, two cases only are considered—the given proposition and its contradictory.

In the exhaustive method, several cases are possible.

But since all of these cases, except one, are shown to be impossible by the *reductio ad absurdum* method, and, hence, are excluded, and since the cases excluded, taken together, and the remaining case may be regarded as contradictories, the exhaustive method may be considered as an extension of the *reductio ad absurdum.*

3. *Example.*

Two triangles which are mutually equilateral are mutually equiangular.

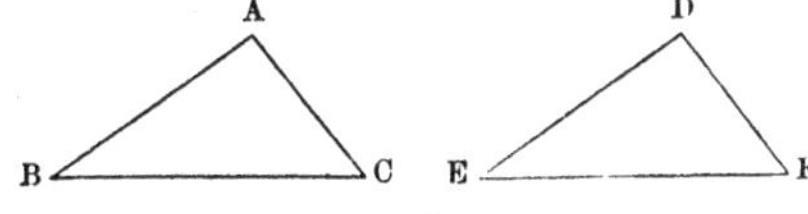

In the triangles A B C and D E F, let A B = D E, A C = D F, and B C = E F, then will the angle A = D, B = E and C = F.

For, taking the angles A and D, there are three and only three cases possible, as follow:

$$A > D,\ A < D, \text{ or } A = D.$$

If $A > D$, $BC > EF$, which is contrary to the hypothesis; $\therefore$ A is not $> D$.

If $A < D$, $BC < EF$, which is contrary to the hypothesis; $\therefore$ A is not $< D$.

Hence, since neither $A > D$ nor $A < D$, $A = D$.

In a similar way it can be proved that $B = E$ and $C = F$.

30. Hamilton's Notation, and Classification of Propositions.

1. *Notation.*
   - : = *all* in affirmative, and *any* in negative propositions.
   - , = *some.*
   - ▶— = *is.*
   - ▶+— = *is not.*

Thus,
- S : ▶— : P is read All S is all P.
- S : ▶+— : P is read Any S is not any P.
- S , ▶+— , P is read Some S is not Some P.

2. *Propositions.*

1*st.* Affirmative.	Toto-total,	(U)	S : ▶— : P
	Toto-partial,	(A)	S : ▶— , P.
	Parti-total,	(Y)	S , ▶— : P.
	Parti-partial,	(I)	S , ▶— , P.
2*d.* Negative.	Toto-total,	(E)	S : ▶+— : P.
	Toto-partial,	(η)	S : ▶+— , P.
	Parti-total,	(O)	S , ▶+— : P.
	Parti-partial,	(ω)	S , ▶+— , P.

3. *The Converse of*

(U) S : ▶— : P = (U) P : ▶— : S.
(A) S : ▶— , P = (Y) P , ▶— : S.
(Y) S , ▶— : P = (A) P : ▶— , S.
(I) S , ▶— , P = (I) P , ▶— , S.
(E) S : ▶+— : P = (E) P : ▶+— : S.
(η) S : ▶+— , P = (O) P , ▶+— : S.
(O) S , ▶+— : P = (η) P : ▶+— , S.
(ω) S , ▶+— , P = (ω) P , ▶+— , S.

4. *Laws of Validity.*

(U) S : ▶— : P. If S and P are coextensive.

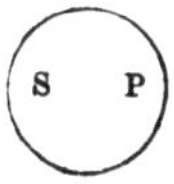

(A) S : ▶— , P. If S is subordinate to P.

(Y) S , ▶— : P. If P is subordinate to S.

(I) S , ▶— , P. If S and P intersect.

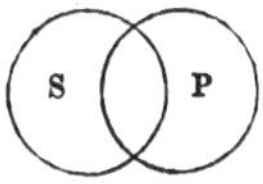

(E) S : ▶+— : P. If S is excluded from P.

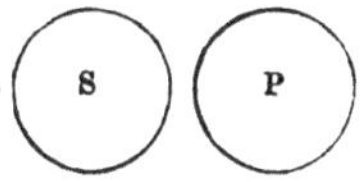

(η) S : ▶+— , P. If S is subordinate to P.

(O) S , ▶+— : P. If P is subordinate to S.

(ω) S , ▶+— , P. If S and P intersect.

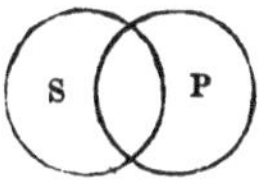

5. *Opposition of Judgments.*

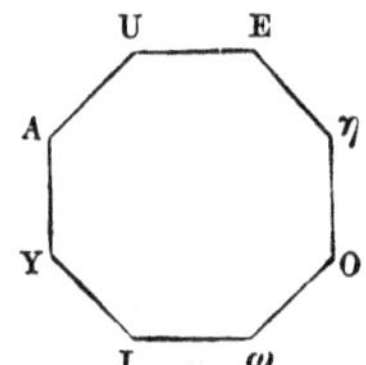

1*st.* Contradictory opposition, existing between (E) and (I).

a. Law.—Both can not be true nor both false.

b. Corollaries.
- *α.* One must be true and the other false
- *β.* The truth of either implies the falsity of the other.
- *γ.* The falsity of either implies the truth of the other.

c. Scholium.—In the classification of categorical propositions before given, it was stated that (A) and (O) are contradictories, as well as (E) and (I). In the present classification, the falsity of (O) does not necessarily imply the truth of (A), for (U) may be true. The difference is owing to this, that in the former classification (A) includes both (U) and (A) of the present classification; hence, the falsity of (O) implies the truth of either (U) or (A).

2*d.* Contrary opposition, existing between (U) and (E), (U) and (η), (U) and (O), (A) and (E), (A) and (O), (Y) and (E), (Y) and (η), one affirmative, the other negative.

a. Law.—Both can not be true, but both may be false.

b. Corollaries.
- α. The truth of either implies the falsity of the other.
- β. The falsity of neither implies the truth of the other.

3*d*. Inconsistent opposition, existing between (U) and (A), (U) and (Y), (A) and (Y), both affirmative.

a. Law.—Both can not be true, but both may be false.

b. Corollaries.
- α. The truth of either implies the falsity of the other.
- β. The falsity of neither implies the truth of the other.

4*th*. Subaltern opposition, existing between (U) and (I), (A) and (I), (Y) and (I), (E) and (η), (E) and (O), (E) and (ω), (η) and (ω), (O) and (ω), both affirmative or both negative.

Laws.
- *a*.
  - α. The truth of the superior implies the truth of the inferior.
  - β. The falsity of the inferior implies the falsity of the superior.
- *b*.
  - α. The falsity of the superior does not imply the falsity of the inferior.
  - β. The truth of the inferior does not imply the truth of the superior.

5*th*. Subcontrary opposition, between (I) and (O).

a. Law.—Both can not be false, but both may be true.

b. Corollaries.
- α. The falsity of either implies the truth of the other.
- β. The truth of neither implies the falsity of the other.

c. Scholium.—The truth of (Y) implies the truth of (O).

6. *Thompson's Criticism on* (η) *and* (ω).

"Why have we ventured, in accordance with the practice, it is believed, of all logicians, to exclude these two, [(η) and (ω)]?

"The answer is, that while Sir William Hamilton gives a table of all *conceivable* cases of negative predication, other logicians have only admitted *actual* cases.

"It is not inconceivable that a man should say, 'No birds are *some* animals' (the η of the Table), and yet such a judgment is never actually made, because it has the semblance only and not the power of a denial. True though it is, it does not prevent our making another judgment of the affirmative kind, from the same terms; and 'All birds are animals' is also true.

"Though such a negative judgment is conceivable, it is useless; and feeling this, men in their daily conversation, as well as logicians in their treatises, have proscribed it.

"But the fruitlessness of a negative judgment, where both terms are particular, is even more manifest; for, 'Some X is not some Y' is true, whatever terms X and Y stand for, and therefore the judgment, as presupposed in every case, is not worth the trouble of forming in any particular one.

"Thus, if I define the composition of common salt by saying 'Common salt is chloride of sodium,' I can not prevent another saying that '*Some* common salt is not *some* chloride of sodium,' because he may mean that the common salt in *this* salt-cellar is not the chloride of sodium in *that*. A judgment of this kind is spurious upon two grounds; it denies nothing, because it does not prevent any of the modes of affirmation; it decides nothing, inasmuch as its truth is presupposed with reference to any pair of conceptions whatever. In a list of *conceivable* modes of predication, these two, [(η) and (ω)], are entitled to a place."

7. *Hamilton's Reply.*

"The thorough-going quantification of the predicate (on demand) in its appliance to negative propositions, is not only allowable, is not only systematic, is not only useful, it is even indispensable. For to speak of its very weakest form, that which I call parti-partial negation, 'Some is not some;' this (besides its own uses) is the form which we naturally employ in dividing a whole of any kind into parts: 'Some A is not some A.' And is this form—that too inconsistently—to be excluded from logic?

"But again (to prove *both* the obnoxious propositions summarily and at once)—what objection, apart from the arbitrary laws of our present logical system, can be taken to the following syllogism?

All man is some animal.
Any man is not (no man is) some animal.
Therefore some animal is not some animal.

"Vary this syllogism of the third figure to any other; it will always be legitimate by nature, if illegitimate to unnatural art. Taking it, however, as it is: the negative minor premise, with its particular predicate, offends logical prejudice. But it is a proposition irrecusable; both as true in itself, and as even practically necessary.

"Its converse, again, is technically allowed; and no proposition can be right of which the converse is wrong. For to say (as has been said from Aristotle downward) that a particular negative proposition is inconvertible, this is merely to confess that the rules of Logicians are inadequate to the truth of logic, and the realities of nature. But this inadequacy is relieved by an unexclusive quantification of the predicate.

"A toto-partial negative can not, therefore, be refused. But if the premises are correct, so likewise must be the conclusion. This, however, is the doubly obnoxious form of a parti-partial negative:

'*Some animal* (man) *is not some animal* (say, brute).'

"Nothing, it may be observed, is more easy than to misapply a form; nothing more easy than to use a weaker, when we are entitled to use a stronger proposition. But from the special and factitious absurdity thus emerging, to infer the general and natural absurdity of the propositional form itself, this is, certainly, not a logical procedure."

8. *De Morgan's Criticism on* (ω).

"The proposition, '*Some X's are not some Y's*,' has no fundamental proposition which denies it. . . . It is what I have called a *spurious* proposition, as long as *either* of its names applies to more than one instance. And the denial of it is as follows: '*There is but one X, and but one Y, and X is Y.*'"

9. *Hamilton's Reply.*

"Here, also, Mr. De Morgan wholly misunderstands the nature and purport of the form which he professes to criticise. He calls it '*a spurious* proposition.' . . . . But in no relation can it ever logically be denominated '*spurious*.'

"For why? Whatever is operative in thought, must be taken into account, and, consequently, be overtly expressible in logic; for logic must be, as it professes to be, an unexclusive reflex of thought, and not merely an arbitrary selection—a series of elegant extracts, out of the forms of thinking.

"What then is the *function* which this form is *peculiarly*—is, indeed, *alone* competent to perform? A parti-partial negative is the proposition in which, and in which exclusively, we declare a whole of any kind to be divisible. '*Some A is not some A*'—this is the judgment of divisibility and of division."

31. Hamilton's Scheme of Figured Syllogisms.

1. *Explanatory Remarks.*

1st. M denotes the middle term, and C and Γ, in the Latin and Greek alphabets, denote the extremes.

2d. *T. B.* denotes total balance, both in propositions and in terms.

3d. *P. B.* denotes partial balance.

4th. *T. U.* denotes total unbalance.

5th. In extension, the broad end of the copula, ▬—, denotes the subject, but in comprehension, the reverse.

6th. In Fig.'s II and III, the double conclusion is denoted by the double copula.

7th. ⌄ denotes that if the premises be converted, the mood is the same.

8th. ⨯ denotes that if the premises be converted, the moods between which it is placed are convertible into each other.

9th. The quantity of the terms of the conclusion are supposed to be the same as in the premises unless otherwise marked.

2. *Figure I.*

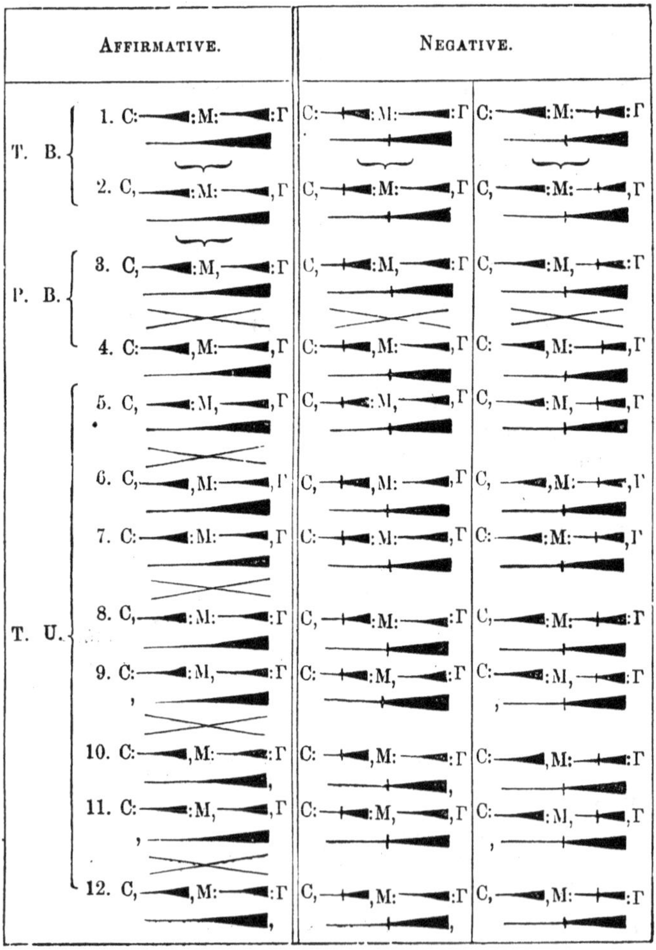

		Affirmative.	Negative.	Negative.
T. B.	1.	C: :M: :Γ	C: :M: :Γ	C: :M: :Γ
T. B.	2.	C, :M: ,Γ	C, :M: ,Γ	C, :M: ,Γ
P. B.	3.	C, :M, :Γ	C, :M, :Γ	C, :M, :Γ
P. B.	4.	C: ,M: ,Γ	C: ,M: ,Γ	C: ,M: ,Γ
T. U.	5.	C, :M, ,Γ	C, :M, ,Γ	C, :M, ,Γ
T. U.	6.	C, ,M: ,Γ	C, ,M: ,Γ	C, ,M: ,Γ
T. U.	7.	C: :M: ,Γ	C: :M: ,Γ	C: :M: ,Γ
T. U.	8.	C, :M: :Γ	C, :M: :Γ	C, :M: :Γ
T. U.	9.	C: :M, :Γ (second line: ,)	C: :M, :Γ	C: :M, :Γ (second line: ,)
T. U.	10.	C: ,M: :Γ (second line: ,)	C: ,M: :Γ (second line: ,)	C: ,M: :Γ
T. U.	11.	C: :M, ,Γ (second line: ,)	C: :M, ,Γ	C: :M, ,Γ (second line: ,)
T. U.	12.	C, ,M: :Γ (second line: ,)	C, ,M: :Γ (second line: ,)	C, ,M: :Γ

3. *Figure II.*

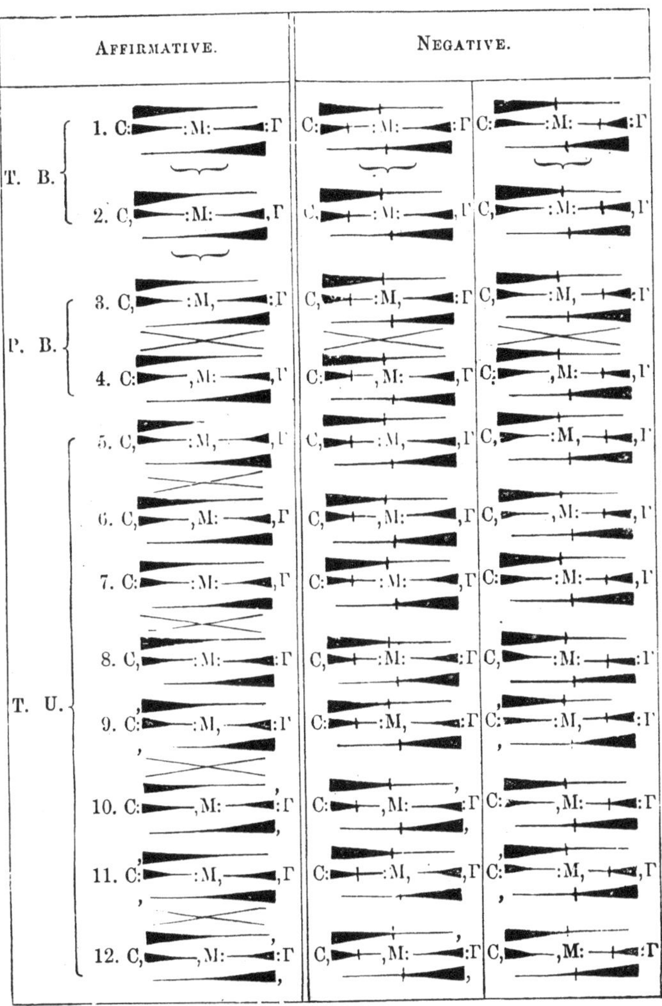

4. *Figure III.*

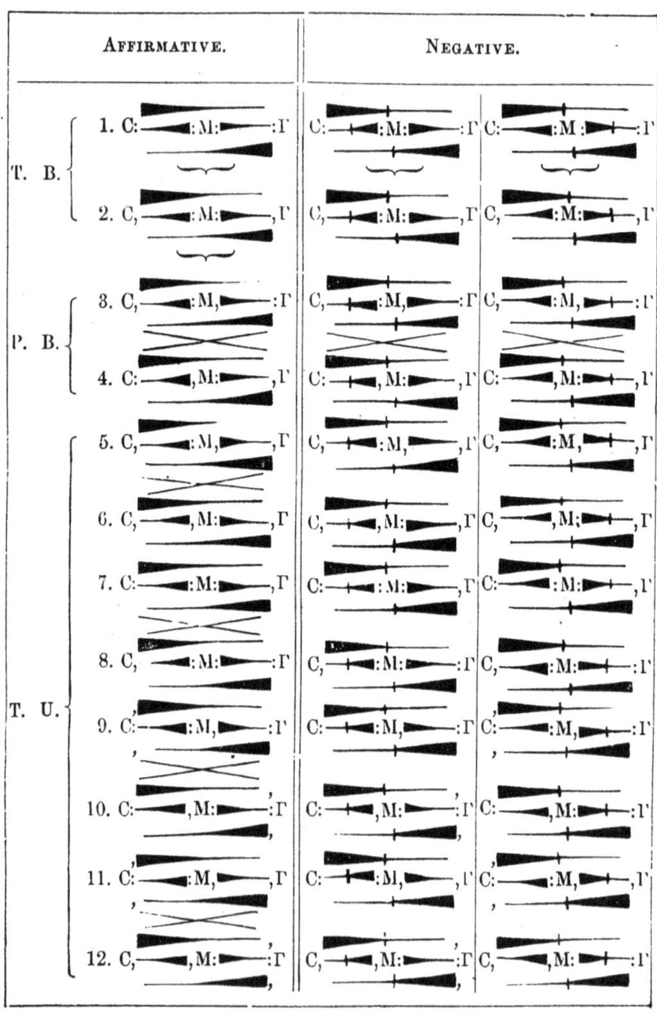

32. Indeterminateness of Language.

One of the greatest obstacles to be surmounted in the development of the science of Logic is the indefinite character of language. Thus, take the four classes of propositions, generally recognized:

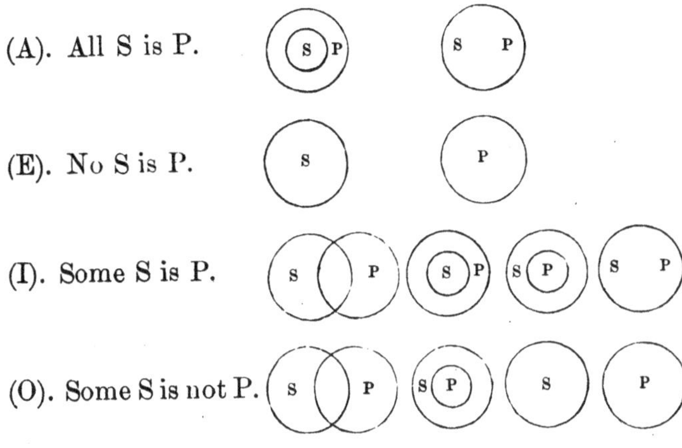

(E) is the only proposition free from ambiguity.

Hamilton's negative propositions, except (E), are not free from ambiguity, as shown thus:

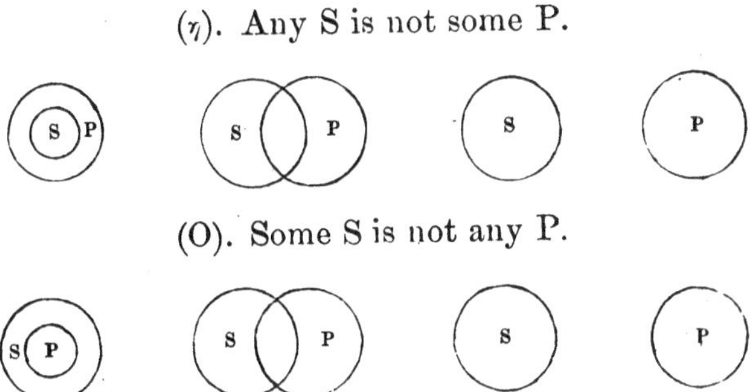

(ω). Some S is not some P

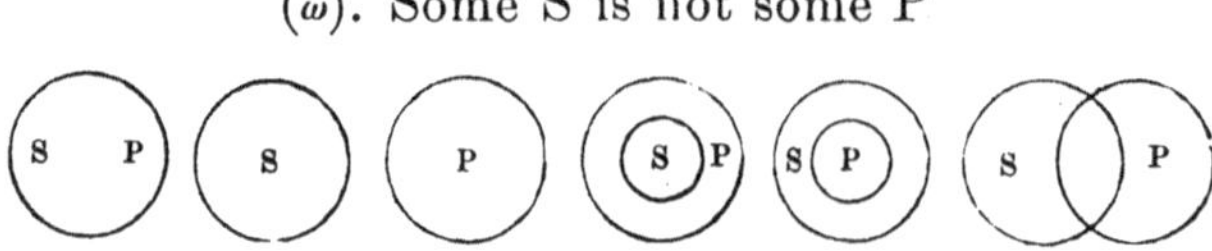

33. Positive Propositions.

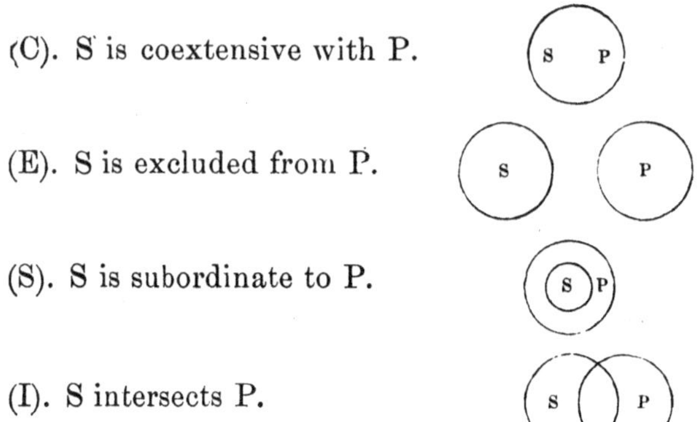

(C). S is coextensive with P.

(E). S is excluded from P.

(S). S is subordinate to P.

(I). S intersects P.

These four propositions express all possible relations of two concepts in extensive quantity.

(A) and (Y), in Hamilton's scheme, both express the relation of subordination. In (A), the subordinate concept is the subject, but in (Y), the subordinate concept is the predicate; but since we can, if we choose, always take the subordinate concept for the subject, we shall treat (A) and (Y) as one.

Let the initial letters, (C), (E), (S), and (I), respectively, denote the relations of coextension, exclusion, subordination, and intersection.

The propositions, (η), (O), (ω), as already shown, are indeterminate, being compatible with two or more of the above relations, and, therefore, indicate either inadequate knowledge or inadequate expression.

34. Positive Syllogisms.

1. *To prove* (*C*).

M is coextensive with P.
M is coextensive with S.
∴ S is coextensive with P.

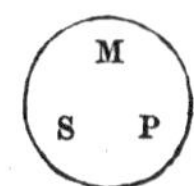

Hence, the relation of coextension is warranted in the conclusion, if the middle is coextensive with each extreme.

2. *To prove* (*E*).

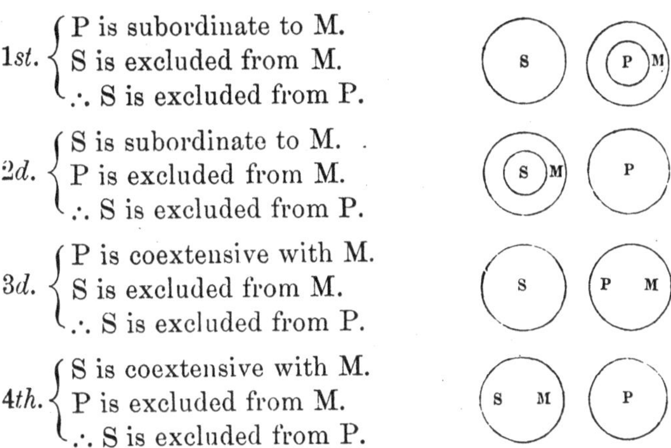

1*st*. { P is subordinate to M.
S is excluded from M.
∴ S is excluded from P. }

2*d*. { S is subordinate to M.
P is excluded from M.
∴ S is excluded from P. }

3*d*. { P is coextensive with M.
S is excluded from M.
∴ S is excluded from P. }

4*th*. { S is coextensive with M.
P is excluded from M.
∴ S is excluded from P. }

Hence, the relation of exclusion is warranted in the conclusion, if one extreme is either subordinate to, or coextensive with, the middle, and the other extreme is excluded from the middle.

3. *To prove* (*S*).

1*st*. { M is subordinate to P.
S is subordinate to M.
∴ S is subordinate to P. }

2*d*. { M is coextensive with P.
S is subordinate to M.
∴ S is subordinate to P.

3*d*. { M is subordinate to P.
S is coextensive with M.
∴ S is subordinate to P.

Hence, the relation of subordination is warranted in the conclusion,

a. If the middle is subordinate to one extreme, and the other extreme is subordinate to the middle.

b. If the middle is coextensive with one extreme, and the other extreme is subordinate to the middle.

c. If the middle is subordinate to one extreme, and the other extreme is coextensive with the middle.

4. *To prove* (*I*).

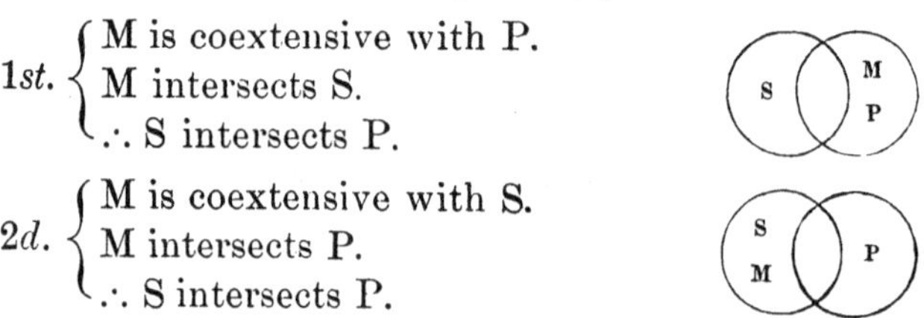

1*st*. { M is coextensive with P.
M intersects S.
∴ S intersects P.

2*d*. { M is coextensive with S.
M intersects P.
∴ S intersects P.

Hence, the relation of intersection is warranted in the conclusion, if the middle term is coextensive with one extreme and intersects the other.

The figure, mood, and order of the premises are mere accidents. Thus, the last syllogism is identical in thought with the following, though the expression is changed:

M intersects P.
S is coextensive with M.
∴ S intersects P.

3. INDUCTION.

1. Definition.

Induction is the process of establishing general propositions from particular cases.

2. Classification.

1*st*. Formal induction, in which the inference is necessitated by the Laws of Thought. Formal induction is of two kinds:

a. Logical induction, in which we reason from all the parts discretively to the whole collectively.

b. Mathematical induction, in which we prove a particular case, and then that if any case is true, the next case is true, and the next, and so on, indefinitely.

2*d*. Real induction, in which we infer that what is true of the parts examined is true of the whole.

3. Position of Induction in Logic.

Formal induction belongs to Pure Logic.
Real induction belongs to Modified Logic.

4. Logical Induction.

1. *Definition.*

Logical induction is the process of reasoning from all the parts to the whole.

2. *Examples.*

1*st*. Inductive syllogisms in extension.

$a.$ $\left\{\begin{array}{l}a, b, c, \text{ are contained under P.}\\ a, b, c, \text{ constitute S.}\\ \therefore \text{ S is contained under P.}\end{array}\right.$

$b.$ $\left\{\begin{array}{l}a, b, c, \text{ constitute M.}\\ \text{S is contained under M.}\\ \therefore \text{ S is contained under } a, b, c.\end{array}\right.$

2*d.* Inductive syllogisms in comprehension.

$a.$ $\left\{\begin{array}{l}\text{S comprehends } a, b, c.\\ a, b, c, \text{ constitute P.}\\ \therefore \text{ S comprehends P.}\end{array}\right.$

$b.$ $\left\{\begin{array}{l}a, b, c, \text{ constitute M.}\\ \text{M comprehends P.}\\ \therefore\ a, b, c, \text{ comprehend P.}\end{array}\right.$

3. *Law.*

What belongs, or does not belong, to all the constituent parts, belongs, or does not belong, to the constituted whole.

5. Mathematical Induction.

1. *Definition.*

Mathematical induction is the process of proving a general proposition, by showing that it holds true for one or more of the first consecutive cases, and then that if it holds for any case, it holds for the next case.

2. *Example.*

The difference of the same powers of two quantities is divisible by the difference of those quantities.

$$\text{Now}\left\{\begin{array}{l}(a-b)\div(a-b)=1.\\ (a^2-b^2)\div(a-b)=a+b.\\ (a^3-b^3)\div(a-b)=a^2+ab+b^2.\\ \cdot\ \cdot\ \cdot\ \cdot\ \cdot\ \cdot\ \cdot\ \cdot\ \cdot\ \cdot\ \cdot\ \cdot\ \cdot\end{array}\right.$$

Let us now divide $a^n - b^n$ by $a - b$.

$$\begin{array}{l|l} a^n - b^n & a - b \\ a^n - a^{n-1}b & \overline{a^{n-1}} \\ \hline a^{n-1}b - b^n = b\,(a^{n-1} - b^{n-1}). & \end{array}$$

Now, it is evident that if $a^{n-1} - b^{n-1}$, which is a factor of the remainder, is divisible by $a - b$, the whole remainder, and consequently the dividend, will be divisible by $a - b$; that is, if $a^{n-1} - b^{n-1}$ is divisible by $a - b$, then $a^n - b^n$ will be divisible by $a - b$; hence, *If the difference of two powers of the same degree is divisible by the difference of the quantities, the difference of the powers one degree greater will be divisible by the difference of the quantities.* But it has already been found that the difference of the powers of the same degree, up to the third power, is divisible by the difference of the quantities, hence, the difference of the fourth powers is divisible by the difference of the quantities, and if the fourth, then the fifth, and so on, to any degree.

6. Day's Theory of Induction.

Let W be a whole of which P is a part and C its complementary part, and A an attribute of P so far as P is W.

Then, what is true of P so far as P is W, is true of C; that is,

Whatever is true of any part of a whole, so far as it is a part of that whole, is true of the complementary part, thus:

P is A so far as P is W.
C is the complementary of P.
∴ C is A.

Objection to this Theory.

That P is A so far as P is W, must mean that P is A, not because A is characteristic of P, but because A is common to all W; that is, because every W is A. *But this is the very thing to be established by induction.* Then the so-called induction is resolved into the deductive syllogism:

Every W is A.
C is W.
∴ C is A.

If every W is not A, it does not follow that C is A, though P is A.

It will not do to reason, Sheep have split hoofs; all other animals taken together are complementary of sheep; ∴ all other animals have split hoofs.

But it may be said that the proposition does not comply with the formula, because it was not said, Sheep, so far as animals, have split hoofs. But this could not be affirmed unless it were known that all animals have split hoofs. It is thus evident that there is no demonstrative reasoning from part to complementary part, except through the whole. The reasoning then becomes deductive. We can indeed reason from part to complementary part, without passing through the whole; but the conclusion is then only probable, and the induction *real* not *formal.*

7. Whately's Theory of Induction.

1. *Signification of Induction.*

"Induction means properly, not the inferring of the conclusion, but the bringing in, one by one, of the instances bearing on the point in question, till a sufficient number has been collected. . . . .

"We do not, strictly, reason *by* Induction, but reason *from* Induction: *i. e.*, from our observations on one, or on several individuals, we draw a conclusion respecting a class they come under; or, in like manner, from several Species to the Genus which comprehends them.

2. *The Inductive Syllogism an Enthymeme with a Suppressed Major.*

"We shall find that the expressed premise of the Enthymeme, viz.: that which contains the statement respecting the individuals is the minor; and that it is the major that is suppressed, as being in all cases substantially the same; viz.: that what belongs to the individual or individuals we have examined, belongs (certainly or probably, as the case may be) to the whole class under which they come.

3. *Necessity of Assuming a Major Premise.*

"It has, however, been urged that what are described as the major premises in drawing inferences from Induction, are resolvable ultimately into an assertion of the 'Uniformity of the laws of Nature,' or some equivalent proposition, and that this is, itself, obtained by Induction; whence it is concluded that there must be at least *one* Induction—and that one, the one on which all others depend—incapable of being exhibited in a syllogistic form.

"But it is evident, and is universally admitted, that in *every case* where an inference is drawn from Induction (unless that name is to be given to a mere random guess without any ground at all) we must form a judgment that the instance or instances adduced are 'sufficient to authorize the conclusion.—that it is 'allowable' to take these instances as a sample warranting an inference respecting the whole class.

"Now, the expression of this judgment in words, is *the very major premise* alluded to. To acknowledge this, therefore, is to acknowledge that all reasoning from induction, *without exception*, does admit of being exhibited in a syllogistic form; and consequently that to speak of one Induction that does not admit of it is a contradiction.

4. *Origin of this Major Premise.*

"Whether the belief in the constancy of Nature's laws—a belief of which no one can divest himself—be intuitive and a part of the constitution of the human mind, as some eminent metaphysicians hold, or acquired, and in what way acquired, is a question foreign to our purpose."

5. *Objections.*

1*st.* The signification of *induction* given by Whately—"the bringing in, one by one, of the instances bearing on the point in question, till a sufficient number has been collected"—is not the meaning generally attached to the word *induction;* for by induction is generally understood the inference that what is true of the parts is true of the whole.

2*d.* Whately's suppressed major premise, "that what belongs to the individual or individuals we have examined, belongs (certainly or probably, as the case may be) to the whole class under which they come," is itself an induction, wider, as to its subject, than the induction expressed by the conclusion, and containing it as a particular case.

How does Whately account for this induction?

He says, "we must form a judgment that the instance or instances adduced are sufficient to authorize the conclusion. . . . . . Now the expression of this judgment in words is the very major premise alluded to." But how is this judgment, which is resolvable into a belief in the constancy of Nature's laws, accounted for? Whately replies, this "is a question foreign to our purpose."

8. Mill's Theory of Induction.

"Whatever be the most proper mode of expressing it, the proposition, that the course of nature is uniform, is the fundamental principle or general axiom of Induction. It would yet be a great error to offer this large generalization as any explanation of the inductive process. On the contrary, I hold it to be itself an instance of induction, and induction by no means of the most obvious kind. Far from being the first induction we make, it is one of the last, or at all events, one of those which are latest in attaining philosophical accuracy. . . . . Yet this principle, though so far from being our earliest induction, must be considered as our warrant for all others, in this sense, that unless it were true, all other inductions would be fallacious."

Remarks.

1. As an explanation of *formal induction* in which the conclusion is demonstrably certain, this theory certainly fails; for, Mr. Mill holds,

1*st.* That the course of nature is uniform, is the fundamental principle or general axiom of Induction.

2*d*. That this principle is itself an induction of by no means the most obvious kind.

3*d*. That far from being the first induction we make, it is one of the last.

4*th*. That this principle must be considered as our warrant for all others.

Then it follows that all other inductions are without warrant, and that this principle is itself without warrant.

2. As an explanation of *real induction* in which the conclusion is only probable, this theory is not liable to objection.

3. The genesis of the induction, that the course of nature is uniform, is as follows: In a particular induction, the uniformity is *observed* in the cases examined, and is, so far, positive. The uniformity observed in the cases examined affords a presumption of the same uniformity in the cases not examined, and this presumption is confirmed as experience enlarges.

Many other inductions are formed and confirmed in the same way.

At length we infer the grand induction that, *The course of nature is uniform.*

4. Real induction affords no absolute certainty.

"Even from the requisites of Induction and Analogy, it is manifest that they bear the stamp of uncertainty; inasmuch as they are unable to determine how many objects or how many characters must be observed, in order to draw the conclusion that the case is the same with all the other objects, or with all the other characters. It is possible only in one way to raise Induction and Analogy from mere probability to complete certainty; viz., to demonstrate that the principles which lie at the root of these processes, and which we have already stated, are either necessary laws of thought, or necessary laws of nature. To demonstrate that they are necessary laws of thought is impossible; for Logic not only does not allow inference from many to all, but expressly rejects it.

"Again, to demonstrate that they are necessary laws of nature is equally impossible. This has, indeed, been attempted, from the uniformity of nature, but in vain. For it is incompetent to evince the necessity of the inference of Induction and Analogy from the fact denominated '*the law of nature*; seeing that this law itself can only be discovered by the way of Induction and Analogy. In this attempted demonstration there is thus the most glaring *petitio principii.* The result which has been previously given remains, therefore, intact: Induction and Analogy guarantee no perfect certainty, but only a high degree of probability, while all probability rests at best upon Induction and Analogy, and nothing else."

These remarks apply to *real induction*, not to *formal.*

9. True's Theory of Induction.

"Its office is to analyze phenomena, to mark the different qualities of objects, and to ascertain their precise effects; but when you have certainly determined what qualities in any case produce what effects, one single instance of causation is sufficient for the widest generalization. Show me the property of the magnet which attracts iron, and I hesitate not to predict that whenever and wherever that quality appears, in like circumstances, it will be followed by the same effect. . . . . Like causes produce like effects."

Remarks.

This explanation may be regarded correct as far as induction relates to the effects of like causes in like circumstances; for whatever there is in the nature of the cause to determine an effect in certain circumstances, a like cause in like circumstances, though numerically different, is, virtually, the same cause in the same circumstances, and the same result would follow.

But induction is not restricted to the inference of effects from causes.

Thus, a naturalist finds that sheep, cattle, deer, and all quadrupeds deficient in upper cutting teeth, so far as he has examined, ruminate; and thus concludes that all quadrupeds thus deficient ruminate. This conclusion may be universally true; but can never be absolutely certain as long as there are quadrupeds in any part of the world that have not been examined.

A man who has noticed that every human being observed by him had but one head, may infer that every human being has but one head; yet this induction might be overthrown by the next show exhibiting a human monstrosity with two heads.

VII. DOCTRINE OF METHOD.

1. Definition.

1. *Definition defined.*

A definition is such a description of an object as will distinguish it from all other objects.

An object is defined by classing it under the genus immediately superior and giving the differential attribute which distinguishes it from its coördinates.

2. *Illustration.*

Thus, triangles, quadrilaterals, pentagons, etc., are coördinate species of the genus, polygon. Then we have the following definitions:

A triangle is a polygon of three sides.

A quadrilateral is a polygon of four sides.

A pentagon is a polygon of five sides.

3. *Object.*

The object of definition is to distinguish the thing defined from other things, and thus to give clearness and precision to thought.

4. *Classification.*

Definitions are of three kinds, *nominal*, *real*, and *genetic*.

1*st*. A nominal definition is a definition of a term. Thus, the word *sphere* signifies a volume bounded by a uniformly curved surface.

2*d*. A real definition is a definition of a thing. Thus, a sphere is a volume bounded by a curved surface all the points of which are equally distant from a point within.

3*d*. A genetic definition is a definition exhibiting the mode of producing the thing. Thus, a sphere is a volume generated by revolving a circle about a diameter.

4. *Laws.*

1*st*. The subject and predicate of a definition must be coextensive. Hence, the simple converse of a definition is true. Thus, a triangle is a polygon of three sides, and conversely, a polygon of three sides is a triangle.

2*d*. There are no exceptions to definitions; for an exception would invalidate the definition.

3*d*. A definition should be precise; that is, omit nothing essential and contain nothing unessential.

4*th*. A definition should be clear; otherwise, it fails in its purpose.

5*th*. A definition should not involve the circle; that is, the predicate should not contain the name of the thing defined, any derivative of that name, or any term whose definition involves the thing defined.

6*th*. A definition should not be made by means of negative or divisive attributes.

7*th*. A definition should not involve a problematic judgment.

5. *Examples of Imperfect Definitions.*

1*st*. "Horses are four-footed animals." The predicate is the definition of quadrupeds, the genus of which horse is a species. We then have the genus given but not the differential quality. The definition, therefore, violates the first law, since the predicate is much more extensive than the subject, including besides horses, sheep, cattle, lions, tigers, etc.

2*d*. "Parallel lines are those which never meet." This definition omits an essential point—that they lie in the same plane, otherwise they might never meet and yet not be parallel.

3*d*. "Parallelograms are quadrilaterals whose oppo site sides are parallel and equal." This definition, though true, contains more than is necessary; for the definition would be complete without the words "and equal," which should, therefore, be omitted as unessential. The equality of the opposite sides follows as a consequence of their parallelism.

4th. "Net-work is any thing decussated or reticulated, with interstices between the intersections." This definition wants clearness; for the terms employed need defining more than the thing defined.

5th. "A law is lawful command." This is a circular definition. So, taken together, are, "Quantity is any thing which may be made the subject of mathematical investigation;" "Mathematics is the science of quantity."

6th. "Industry is not honesty." This does not tell what industry is, but what it is not.

7th. "Patriotism is a moral, social, or political virtue." This is too indeterminate.

8th. "A miracle is an effect or event contrary to the established constitution or course of things, or a sensible suspension or controlment of, or deviation from, the known laws of nature, wrought either by the immediate act, or by the concurrence, or by the permission of God, for the proof or evidence of some particular doctrine, or in attestation of the authority of some particular person." Not content with the discrimination of a miracle from all other phenomena, the writer adds his theory of miracles, telling by whom wrought and for what purpose.

2. Division.

1. *Definition.*

Division is the resolution of an extensive concept into the subordinate concepts contained under it.

2. *Object.*

1st. The primary object of division is to obtain extensive distinctness.

2d. The secondary object of division is to obtain completeness.

3. *Classification.*

1st. As to nature.

a. Physical or real division, when the parts are actually separated.

b. Metaphysical or ideal division, when the parts are separated in thought.

2d. As to the number of coördinate members.

a. A dichotomy, when there are only two coördinate members.

b. A polytomy, when there are more than two coordinate members.

α. A trichotomy is a polytomy of three members.

β. A tetrachotomy is a polytomy of four members.

4. *The Principle of Division.*

The principle of division is that attribute in reference to which the division is made.

It is evident that the same class may be divided in reference to different principles.

The following is an illustration:

Triangles may be divided,

- *1st.* As to the sides.
  - *a.* Scalene.
  - *b.* Isoceles.
    - *α.* Bi-equilateral.
    - *β.* Tri-equilateral.
- *2d.* As to the angles.
  - *a.* Right angled.
  - *b.* Oblique angled.
    - *α.* Acute angled.
    - *β.* Obtuse angled.

5. *Law.*

The Law of Contradictories regulates division.

Thus, triangles, as to their angles, are right angled or non-right angled, that is, oblique angled.

Strictly, every logical division gives a dichotomy. Sometimes, however, one of the two coördinate members is omitted and its parts substituted in its place.

Thus, in dividing triangles as to their angles, instead of taking the two coördinate members, right angled and oblique angled, we may omit the oblique angled, and substitute in its place its parts—acute angled and obtuse angled. Thus, giving the following classification:

Triangles. { Right angled.
Acute angled.
Obtuse angled.

6. *Rules.*

1*st.* Every division should be made in reference to some principle.

2*d.* Every division should be made in reference to only one principle.

3*d.* The principle of division should be an actual determinate attribute of the divided class.

4*th.* The principle of division should be selected with reference to the object to be accomplished.

5*th.* Each of the members must be less than the class divided.

6*th.* The sum of the members must be equal to the class divided.

7*th.* The members must be mutually exclusive.

8*th.* The members must be coördinate.

9th. The divisions and subdivisions must proceed continuously; that is, each member must be immediately subordinate to the concept under which it is placed.

7. *Faulty Divisions.*

1st. Human actions are necessary or free or useful or detrimental.

2d. Triangles are divided into right angled, scalene, and acute angled.

3d. Parallelograms are divided into squares and rectangles.

4th. Human conduct is good or bad.

5th. Philosophy is divided into theoretical, practical, and moral.

3. Analysis.

1. *Definition.*

Analysis is the resolution of a comprehensive concept into the attributes contained in it.

2. *Object.*

1st. The primary object of analysis is to obtain comprehensive distinctness.

2d. The secondary object is to obtain completeness.

3. *Rule.*

Take the attributes common to all of the coördinate members of the genus immediately containing the species, or the species containing the individual, together with the characteristic attributes of the species or individual to be analyzed.

It will greatly aid in attaining comprehensive distinctness to begin with *being*, the highest genus, and proceed by *division*, retaining the member containing the given concept under it, taking, at each step, the attributes of the genus, and the characteristics of the retained member, till the given concept is reached.

4. Argumentation.

1. *Definition.*

Argumentation is a process of reasoning the object of which is to establish the truth of a proposition.

2. *Results.*

By argumentation truth is proved, the concatenation and dependence of thoughts are ascertained, and the congruence or harmony of thoughts is secured.

3. *Elements.*

1*st*. The conclusion or proposition to be proved.

2*d*. The premises or grounds of proof.

3*d*. The relation between the premises and the conclusion.

4. *Conditions.*

1*st*. The premises must be known to be true.

2*d*. The premises must be so related to each other and to the conclusion as to necessitate the conclusion.

5. *Classification.*

1*st*. As to validity.

a. Valid, when the conclusion is proved.

b. Invalid, when the conclusion is not proved.

2*d*. As to the medium of proof.

a. Mediate, when there is a middle term.

b. Immediate, when there is no middle term.

3*d*. As to form.

a. Regular, when stated in due form.
b. Irregular, when not stated in due form.

4*th*. As to method.

a. Direct, when the conclusion is proved directly.
b. Indirect, when the conclusion is proved indirectly.

5*th*. As to the order of procedure.

a. Inductive, when the procedure is from the parts to the whole.
b. Deductive, when the procedure is from the whole to the parts.

6*th*. As to logical quantity.

a. Extensive, when the reasoning is in extensive quantity.
b. Comprehensive, when the reasoning is in comprehensive quantity.

7*th*. As to figure.

a. Figured, when the terms are related as subject and predicate.
b. Unfigured, when the terms are not related as subject and predicate.

8*th*. As to the order of the premises and conclusion.

a. Analytic, when the conclusion is stated first.
b. Synthetic, when the premises are stated first.

9*th*. As to simplicity.

a. Simple, when there is but one syllogism.
b. Compound, when two or more syllogisms are combined.

10*th*. As to cogency.

a. Demonstrative, when the truth of the conclusion is absolute.

b. Probable, when the truth of the conclusion is not absolute.

11*th*. As to completeness.

a. Complete, when all the parts are fully stated.

b. Incomplete, when all the parts are not fully stated.

12*th*. As to the nature of the premises.

a. *A priori*, when the premises are intuitive principles.

b. *A posteriori*, when the premises are established by experience.

13*th*. As to the fundamental laws of thought involved.

a. Categorical, when the form is determined by the Law of Identity or the Law of Conflictives.

b. Hypothetical, when the form is determined by the Law of Reason and Consequent.

c. Disjunctive, when the form is determined by the Law of Contradictories.

d. Dilemmatic, when the hypothetic and disjunctive forms are combined.

6. *Rules*.

1*st*. Nothing is to be assumed to be true which is not known to be true; that is, "nothing is to be begged, borrowed, or stolen."

2*d*. No proposition is to be employed as a premise the truth of which depends on the conclusion.

3*d*. A proposition must not be used to prove itself.

4th. No leap or hiatus must be made.

5th. A different proposition must not be proved in place of the given proposition.

VIII. MODIFIED LOGIC.

1. Truth.

1. *Definition.*

Truth is the harmony of thought with its object.

2. *Classification.*

1st. Formal truth, the harmony of thought with the form of thought.

a. Logical truth, the harmony of thought with the necessary laws of thought.

b. Mathematical truth, the harmony of thought with the necessary relations of quantity.

2d. Real truth, the harmony of thought with its matter.

a. Physical truth, the harmony of thought with external phenomena.

b. Metaphysical truth, the harmony of thought with the necessary facts of mind.

c. Psychological truth, the harmony of thought with the contingent facts of mind.

3. *Criterion.*

The criterion of truth is intuition or demonstration necessitating certainty; for, if certainty exists, all doubt is dispelled; for to doubt what we necessarily think is contradictory and impossible.

2. Error.

1. *Definition.*

Error is the opposite of truth; and is, therefore, the want of harmony between thought and its object.

2. *Distinguished from Ignorance and Illusion.*

Ignorance is negation of knowledge, error is positive pretense to knowledge.

An illusion is a deceptive appearance arising from certain conditions and affections in the thinking subject. Thus, pressure on the eye causes spots to appear.

3. *Sources.*

1*st.* Ignorance, leading to the assumption of the non-existence of that of which we are ignorant.

2*d.* Illusion, leading to the assumption that the deceptive appearance is an objective reality.

3*d.* The disturbing influence of the will or the sensibilities.

4*th.* A defect in the object of knowledge.

5*th.* Circumstances, nationality, social relations, educational prejudices.

6*th.* The constitutional peculiarities of the individual.

7*th.* The defects inherent in language.

8*th.* The nature of the knowledge about which thought is conversant.

4. *Remedies.*

1*st.* General intelligence.

2*d.* A symmetrical and thorough education.

3*d.* A proper application of logical principles.

3. Investigation.

1. *Definition.*

Investigation is that intellectual process which has for its object the discovery of truth.

2. *Methods.*

Experience, observation, experiment, hypothesis, induction, analogy.

1. Experience.

1. *Definition.*

Experience is the apprehension of external or internal phenomena through perception and consciousness.

2. *Kinds.*

1*st.* Personal; that is, our own experience.

2*d.* Foreign; that is, the experience of others.

Personal experience is more certain; foreign, more extensive.

3. *Relation to Knowledge.*

All knowledge begins with experience.

2. Observation and Experiment.

1. *Definition.*

1*st.* Observation is the voluntary attention of the intellect directed to a certain object.

2*d.* Experiment is an extension of observation effected by means of instruments or apparatus by which we vary the circumstances of the phenomena.

2. *Conditions to be observed.*

1*st*. Subjective: The mind should be in vigorous condition, self-possessed, and free from prepossession, partiality, or prejudice.

2*d*. Objective: The attention must be directed to the thing observed, which is to be divided and subdivided, if necessary, till the perceptions become clear, and all foreign or adventitious matter is to be excluded.

3. *Rules for Procedure.*

1*st*. Observe, analyze, compare, and classify the phenomena.

2*d*. Determine the conditions requisite to their reality.

3*d*. Ascertain the causes of the phenomena.

4*th*. Discover the laws of the phenomena.

5*th*. Make a record of the results.

4. *Remark.*

A compliance with these rules will require also the application of the following methods of investigation.

3. Hypothesis.

1. *Definition.*

An hypothesis is a supposition made to account for certain phenomena.

2. *Relation to the Phenomena.*

1*st*. An hypothesis that accounts for the phenomena may be regarded, provisionally, as the true explanation.

2*d.* The only possible hypothesis that accounts for the phenomena must be regarded as the true explanation.

4. Real Induction.

1. *Definition.*

Real induction is the process of reasoning from some of the parts to the whole.

2. *Varieties.*

1*st.* Individual induction; when the parts are individuals of which the whole is the species.

2*d.* Special induction; when the parts are species of which the whole is the genus.

3. *Conditions.*

1*st.* The partial judgments from which the general judgment is inferred must be of the same quality; that is, all affirmative or all negative.

2*d.* That a requisite number of parts be observed. This condition is necessarily somewhat vague, since the number required will vary with the circumstances.

4. *Nature of the General Proposition.*

The general proposition inferred by induction is to be regarded only as probable. This probability is increased in proportion,

1*st.* To the number and variety of the objects observed.

2*d.* To the accuracy of the observations and comparisons.

3*d.* To the clearness and precision of the agreement.

4th. To the thoroughness of search for exceptions, none being found.

5. Analogy.

1. *Definition.*

Analogy is the process of reasoning from the similarity of objects in certain respects to their similarity in other respects.

2. *Conditions.*

1st. The objects observed must agree in certain respects.

2d. The attributes observed must not be all negative or all accidental.

3. *Nature of the Conclusion.*

The conclusion is only probable. The probability of the conclusion is increased in proportion,

1st. To the number and accuracy of the observations.

2d. To the number of congruent attributes.

3d. To the importance of the congruent attributes.

4. *Example.*

P has the attributes *a*, *b*, *c*, and *d*.
Q has the attributes *a*, *b*, *c*.
∴ Q probably has the attribute *d*.

5. *Refutation.*

This argument can be refuted if it can be shown either,

1st. That *d* is the effect of some attribute which is in P but not in Q.

2*d*. That there are present with P and absent from Q certain circumstances which are indispensable conditions of *d*.

3*d*. That Q has some attribute incompatible with *d*.

4*th*. That the circumstances attending Q prevent the existence of *d*.

6. *Illustration.*

The earth is an opaque solid, nearly spherical, derives light and heat from the sun, and is inhabited.

The moon is an opaque solid, nearly spherical, derives light and heat from the sun.

∴ The moon is probably inhabited.

The points of difference, that the moon is smaller, more rugged, revolves on its axis but once in twenty-eight days, has no atmosphere and no water, present a counter probability that the moon is not inhabited.

If the points of agreement are equally likely to be the conditions of life, the probability that the moon is inhabited would vary directly as the number of such points of agreement.

But, since some of the circumstances wanting on the moon, such as air and water, are indispensable conditions of life on the earth, we must conclude, either that the moon is not inhabited at all, or that the conditions on which life depends on the moon are totally different from the conditions on which life depends on the earth. The conditions of life on the moon being, therefore, different from those on the earth, if they exist at all, the more points of resemblance established between the moon and the earth, the indispensable conditions which exist on the earth being wanting, the less the probability of the supposed different conditions, and, consequently, the less the probability that the moon is inhabited.

7. *Uses of Analogical Argument.*

If not refuted, it may be usefully employed,

1*st.* To show the reasonableness of the conclusion.

2*d.* To remove prejudice.

3*d.* To silence objections.

4*th.* To prepare the mind for direct argument.

8. *Induction and Analogy compared.*

1*st.* By induction we infer that an attribute belonging to many objects of a class, belongs to all the objects of that class.

2*d.* By analogy we infer that objects agreeing in certain respects, agree in other respects.

3*d.* They agree in the fact that they give only probable conclusions, and that the degree of probability may vary between the limits, impossibility and certainty, without ever reaching either limit.

6. Examples of Investigation.

1. *Method of Agreement.*

The effect of A B C is *a b c*.
The effect of A D E is *a d e*.

∴ { *b* and *c* are not effects of A.
d and *e* are not effects of A.
a is not the effect of either B C or D E.
a is the effect of A.

2. *Method of Difference.*

1st. { The effect of A B C is $a\ b\ c$.
The effect of B C is $b\ c$.
∴ The effect of A is a.

2d. { The cause of $a\ b\ c$ is A B C.
The cause of $b\ c$ is B C.
∴ The cause of a is A.

3. *Method of Residues.*

{ A B C is the cause of $a\ b\ c$.
B is the cause of b.
C is the cause of c.
∴ A is the cause of a.

4. *Method of Concomitant Variations.*

Let A′, A″ be variations of A, and a', a'' variations of a.

{ A B C is the cause of $a\ b\ c$.
A′ B C is the cause of $a'\ b\ c$.
A″ B C is the cause of $a''\ b\ c$.
∴ A is the cause of a.

This method is especially valuable in case of permanent causes; that is, when cases can not be found free from their influence, as in the case of the connection of the moon with the phenomena of the tides.

Thus, though we can not remove the earth from the influence of the moon, yet we can observe the variations in the position of the moon with respect to the earth and the concomitant variations of the tides. The influence of the moon in the production of the tides is hence determined.

In a similar manner the influence of the sun is determined.

IX. FALLACIES.

Definition and Classification.

A fallacy is an invalid intellectual process.

There are three classes of fallacies, *assumptions*, *sophisms*, and *aberrancies*.

1. Assumptions.

1. *Definition.*

An assumption is that which is taken as true without evidence.

2. *Ground of Invalidity.*

Assumptions may be true or false; but, resting on no basis of evidence, they are, in both cases, invalid, not because known to be false, but because not known to be true.

To assume an assumption false, because of its lack of evidence, would be a procedure as invalid as to assume it true.

3. *Classes.*

1*st*. *Assumptions arising from non-observation or mal-observation.*

The common source of these is *want of attention.*

Failing to notice many things, we are liable to assume their non-existence.

Other things, not wholly overlooked, are, from inattention, misapprehended, and, assuming them to be what they are not, we are involved in confusion. Of how many may it be said, "Having eyes, they see not." A very amusing and instructive example of this is found in a dialogue entitled "Eyes and No

Eyes." Two persons passed over the same route the same day; but to one the journey was wholly devoid of interest, while to the other, objects of interest abounded on every hand, a glowing account of which he gave, greatly to the edification and astonishment of his unobserving friend.

2*d*. *Assumptions arising from prejudice.* This is a fruitful source of assumptions, and it is very difficult to divest ourselves of its influence, yet we are loth to admit that we are, in any degree, subject to its control. "Can any good thing come out of Nazareth?" is the expression of intensified prejudice.

From too high an opinion of ourselves, too low an opinion of others, ruling desires, nationality, party, church, or society relations, education, and association, arise prejudices leading to assumptions which vitiate our judgments and involve us in error.

The antidotes which neutralize the poison of prejudice are, an honest heart, a good disposition, a love for truth, due caution, and patient investigation.

3*d*. *Assumption that what is true of ourselves is true of others.* How slow is a man habitually governed by selfish considerations to believe that another who has done a noble deed to bless humanity was actuated by disinterested motives! How clearly is the true character of a person often revealed by the judgment which he passes upon another! Conscious of his own dishonesty or impurity, he assumes that others are as dishonest and vile as he.

4*th*. *Assumptions arising from superstition.* Superstition has produced a numerous brood from its mythologies, oracles, omens, witchcrafts, apparitions, ghosts, fairies, signs, and charms.

Though superstition is less potent now than formerly, it has not yet altogether lost its influence, as is indicated by such sayings as these:

"If it rains the first Sunday of a month, it will rain every Sunday."

"If you first see the new moon over your right shoulder, you will have good luck for that month."

5*th. Assumptions arising from hasty generalization.* Finding of a certain nation a few individuals of a certain character, some hastily assume that to be the character of the whole nation. I well remember the time when I judged the whole English nation to be bigoted, narrow-minded, conceited, and overbearing, because that was the character of the few with whom I happened to be acquainted; but I have since learned, that among the English are the large-hearted and noble, an honor to humanity and to God.

The same fallacy is quite prevalent in reference to the subject of education. The failures of graduates, on the one hand, are pointed out as exhibiting the inutility of education, not recollecting that much worthless timber is sent to college, and yet, though not one of a thousand of the nation is a graduate of a college, the majority of the prominent public men have pursued the prescribed course of study, and have received the honor of graduation.

On the other hand, the splendid achievements of a Franklin, or the sublime deeds of a Washington, are referred to as examples showing that education is not essential to the highest success, forgetting that these men were gifted with the noblest endowments, and that their struggles with difficulties developed their powers and enabled them to achieve immortal renown.

But how rare such cases! Shall we take such men, raised up and endowed by Providence to accomplish a great purpose, as indicating the principles which should guide us in the great work of education? Then, although there might be a few great men, the mass of mankind would sink into the darkness of barbarism.

This tendency to form hasty general conclusions is exhibited in other instances. Thus, a man confessedly below par accidentally becomes rich. Forthwith his neighbors exclaim, "Fortune favors fools." They cast about for similar instances and are sure to be successful in finding or imagining them. They hence conclude that success is bestowed by a caprice of fortune, forgetting the multitude of instances in which ignorance and imbecility are attended with their legitimate fruits—poverty and degradation, and those cases in which intelligent, well-directed effort is crowned with the most triumphant success.

The ground of the fallacy seems to be this: These cases are contrary to what might naturally be expected, and, hence, their occurrence makes a strong impression, not likely to be forgotten, while the reverse cases, though far more numerous, are looked upon as matters of course, and, making but a slight impression, are overlooked, and the general conclusion is drawn from the far less numerous, though more striking exceptional cases.

6th. Assumption that appearances correspond to realities. The ancients could not believe that the earth was round, or that it moved, because apparently contrary to the evidence of their senses. They could, however, readily believe that the sun, and the moon, and the stars revolved round the earth every twenty-four hours, because such is the appearance.

When the moon is viewed through flying clouds,

it seems to be moving and the clouds seem at rest. But is that apparent motion the real motion of the moon? On a certain occasion, a company of boys were looking at the moon through such fleecy, flying clouds. All, save one, decided that the moon was running away, and were deeply indignant at what they called his stupidity, when he affirmed that the apparent motion of the moon was owing to the real motion of the clouds. "Have n't we eyes? Can 't we see?" The other boy, with the sagacity of a philosopher, conducted his companions to a tree and directed them to look at the moon through the branches. To their utter astonishment, the moon maintained its position, and the clouds sailed far away. That boy became the great philosopher Gassendi.

7th. Assumptions originating in preconceived opinions. When Copernicus advanced his theory respecting the motion of the earth, his opponents met him with the objection that, if it did move, a stone let fall from the top of a tower would not strike the ground at the foot of the tower, but at a little distance from it, in a direction contrary to the motion of the earth, just as a ball, as they affirmed, let fall from the mast-head, while the ship is sailing, does not strike the deck at the foot of the mast, but nearer the stern of the vessel.

The Copernicans met this objection, not by denying the spurious fact, and proving, as they should have done, by direct experiment, that a ball let fall from the mast-head does not strike the deck nearer the stern than the foot of the mast, but by saying that the ball was no part of the ship, and that the motion forward was not natural either to the ship or to the ball, while, on the other hand, the stone was a part of the tower, and, therefore, the motions which were natural to the earth were natural to the stone, and, therefore, it should strike the ground precisely at the foot of the tower.

The opponents of Copernicus were wrong in assuming that if the earth revolved, the stone would strike the ground a little distance from the foot of the tower in a direction contrary to the motion of the earth, whereas the reverse is true; for the stone falling from the top of the tower has the same motion eastward, and since the top of the tower is farther from the axis of rotation than the foot, its motion eastward is greater; consequently, the stone would fall a little to the east of the foot of the tower.

The following experiments, the account of which is taken from Loomis's Astronomy, fully confirm the theory: The mean of twelve trials from a tower 256 *ft.* high, at Bologna, gave .74 *in.* deviation to the east, and .47 *in.* to the south. The mean of thirty-one experiments from a tower 250 *ft.* high, at Hamburg, gave .35 *in.* deviation to the east, and .11 *in.* to the south. The mean of one hundred and six trials at Freyburg, in a mine whose depth was 520 *ft.*, gave 1.12 *in.* deviation east and .17 *in.* south.

Prof. Loomis remarks: "The deviation south is not accounted for by the theory." But this deviation can be accounted for thus: The top of the tower, at any instant, is moving in a vertical plane tangent to the circle of latitude drawn through the foot of the tower, and since this tangent plane intersects the surface of the earth in a line which continually deviates to the south of the circle of latitude for all places north of the equator, and to the north for all places south of the equator, it follows that in north latitude the deviation should be both east and south, in south latitude both east and north, and at the equator east only.

The importance of testing theory by experiment, where it is practicable, is strikingly exemplified in the long prevailing doctrine of the ancients respecting falling bodies. According to the Aristotelians, "Heavy bodies must fall quicker than light ones; for weight is the cause of their fall, and the weight of the greater body is the greater." How easy it would have been, by direct experiment, to settle the question effectually! A large stone and a small one might have been dropped, simultaneously, over a precipice, and they would have been found to strike the ground at the same instant.

8*th. Assumptions pertaining to space.* By a rational mind unbiased by theory, space is apprehended as a reality, independent and absolute. It is not apprehended as a mere conception of the mind, or law of thought, nor as substance, material or spiritual, nor as the attribute of substance, nor as the object of creation or destruction. Reason apprehends space as infinite extension, the room for the universe.

The idea of space, then, is a rational intuition, of which the idea of body is the chronological antecedent; that is, in the order of time, the idea of body is developed in the intelligence before that of space. But, immediately, on the perception of body, reason apprehends the reality of space as its necessary logical antecedent.

It is intuitively certain that if there is body, there must be room in which the body exists.

We attain to the idea of space through that of body; but space itself, when once apprehended by reason, is known as absolute, infinite extension. Were all bodies swept from existence, there would still be space. Were all spiritual existences annihilated, space would still stretch forth in all directions, without limit, on, forever on, an infinite abyss.

Certain philosophers, among whom is Hamilton, hold that the infinite is not an object of knowledge. Their doctrine is, to use a Hamiltonian expression, "*The infinite is unthinkable.*" They resolve the notion of infinite space into a mental impotency to conceive that space has bounds.

Hamilton holds that the idea of space involves contradictions. In order not to misrepresent his views, we quote his words:

"Extension, then, may be viewed as a whole or as a part; and in each aspect, it affords us two incogitable contradictories. 1°. Taking it as a whole: Space, it is evident, must either be limited, that is, have an end, a circumference; or unlimited, that is, have no end, no circumference. These are contradictory suppositions; both, therefore, can not, but one must, be true.

"Now let us try positively to comprehend, positively to conceive, the possibility of either of these two mutually exclusive alternatives. Can we represent or realize in thought, extension as absolutely limited? in other words, can we mentally hedge round the whole of space, conceive it absolutely bounded, that is, so that beyond its boundary, there is no outlying, no surrounding space? This is impossible. Whatever compass of space we may inclose by any limitation of thought, we shall find that we have no difficulty in transcending these limits. Nay, we shall find that we can not but transcend them; for we are unable to think any extent of space except as within a still ulterior space, of which let us think, till the powers of thinking fail, we can never reach the circumference. We may, therefore, lay down the first extreme as inconceivable, we can not think space as limited.

"Let us now consider its contradictory: can we comprehend the possibility of infinite or unlimited space? To suppose this is a direct contradiction in terms; it is to comprehend the incomprehensible. We think, we conceive, we comprehend a thing, only as we think it within or under something else; but to do this of the infinite, is to think the infinite as finite, which is contradictory and absurd."

This view is here presented in its full force. To comprehend signifies to circumscribe. The infinite can not, therefore, be comprehended, for this would make it finite. But let us not be deceived by a word. Though the infinite is to be regarded as incomprehensible, from the fact that it can not be referred to something greater under which it is classed, yet it does not follow that it is unknowable.

The distinction between the comprehensible and the knowable is clearly shown by Hamilton himself. We quote from his Philosophy of Common Sense:

"To make the comprehensibility of a datum of consciousness the criterion of its truth, would be, indeed, the climax of absurdity. For, the primary data of consciousness, as themselves the conditions under which all else is comprehended, are, necessarily, themselves incomprehensible. We know and can know, only that they *are*, not how they can be. To ask how an immediate fact of consciousness is possible, is to suppose that we have another consciousness, before and above that human consciousness, concerning whose mode of operation we inquire. Could we do this, verily, we should be as gods."

This is clear and to the point. That is comprehensible which can be referred to something else containing it. But intuitions, being ultimate, can not be referred to ulterior principles which comprehend them. They are, therefore, incomprehensible. But because incomprehensible, they are not, therefore, unknowable; for, in the language of Hamilton, "we know that they *are*, not how they can be."

But how do we know that space is infinite? This knowledge is not to be resolved into a mental *impotency* to conceive that space has bounds, but rather into a *potency* to apprehend that it can have no bounds; for, as Hamilton has well said, "Whatever compass of space we may inclose by any limitation of thought, we shall find that we have no difficulty in transcending these limits. Nay, we shall find that we can not but transcend them; for we are unable to think any extent of space except as within a still ulterior space."

Space, then, has no limits beyond which there is not ulterior space; and as we can not but transcend any limit, we know that space is not finite. But, by the law of contradictories, one of two contradictory propositions must be true, and but one can be true. If, then, one is known to be false, the other is known to be true. But we know it to be false that space is finite; therefore we know it to be true that space is infinite.

In reference to the objection that we can not comprehend the infinite, because that would make it finite, we reply that we indeed grant that we can not form, in the imagination, a picture of the infinite; for a picture necessarily has outlines or boundaries, or, in other words, is finite. But because the infinite can not be represented in the imagination, it does not follow that it can not be known by the reason. Our knowledge of the infinite, then, is not a representation by the imagination, but an intuition by the reason. Hamilton's contradictions thus arose from referring the infinite to the wrong faculty.

If the genesis of the notion that space is infinite is the fact that it can not be conceived to be finite, then there is an equally good reason for the notion that space is finite, from the fact that it can not be conceived to be infinite. If one is a sufficient warrant for the notion that it is infinite, the other is a sufficient warrant for the notion that it is finite. Then we have sufficient warrant for the contradictory notions, that space is infinite, and that space is finite.

The nearly universal notion that space is infinite must lead us to conclude that the origin of this opinion is not the fact that it can not be conceived to be finite; for then the notion ought to be equally universal that space is finite, from the fact that it can not be conceived to be infinite.

The mere negation of power to conceive a proposition to be true is not a warrant for the inference that its contradictory is true; but this warrant is found in the positive knowledge, gained by intuition, demonstration, or experience, that the proposition can not be true.

Not only is there the want of power to conceive space as finite, which is, of course, a mere negation, an impotence, but there is positive power to see that it can not be finite. Then by the law of contradictories, it must be infinite.

2. Sophisms.

1. *Definition.*

A sophism is an invalid argument.

2. *Classes.*

1*st*. *Formal fallacies*. These are, the undistributed middle, illicit process, negative premises, particular premises, affirmative premises and a negative conclusion, one negative premise and an affirmative conclusion, one particular premise and a universal conclusion, and ambiguous middle, which have already been discussed.

2*d*. *Petitio principii*, the begging of the question. This fallacy consists in deducing the conclusion from premises one of which depends on the conclusion. According to Mr. Mill, every syllogism involves this fallacy. He says: "It must be granted that in every syllogism, considered as an argument to prove the conclusion, there is a *petitio principii*. When we say,

All men are mortal,
Socrates is a man,
∴ Socrates is mortal;

it is unanswerably urged by the adversaries of the syllogystic theory, that the proposition, Socrates is mortal, is presupposed in the more general assumption, All men are mortal: that we can not be assured of the mortality of all men, unless we were previously certain of the mortality of every individual man; that if it be still doubtful whether Socrates, or any other individual you choose to name, be mortal or not, the same degree of uncertainty must hang over the assertion, All men are mortal: that the general principle, instead of being given as evidence of the particular case, can not itself be taken for true without exception, until every shadow of doubt which could affect any case comprised within it is dispelled by evidence *aliundè;* and then what remains for the syllogism to prove? that, in short, no reasoning from generals to particulars can, as such, prove any thing: since from a general principle you can not infer any particulars, but those which the principle itself assumes as foreknown."

In grappling with this famous objection to the syllogistic theory, we shall demonstrate that so far from it being true, "That the general principle, instead of being given as evidence of the particular case, can not itself be taken for true without exception, until every shadow of doubt which could affect any case comprised within it is dispelled by evidence *aliundè*," it is a fact that the general principle, though not of course true unless every particular case included under it is true, is itself often established, in its utmost generality, without any reference to the particular cases involved. Do we establish the general principle that, *Any term of an Arithmetical Progression is equal to the first term plus the number of the term minus one into the common difference*, by examining all of the cases involved? Do we not, in fact, establish the general principle without reference to the particular cases?

Thus, let a denote the first term and d the common difference of any increasing arithmetical progression, then from the law of the series, the terms will be,

$$a,\ a+d,\ a+2\,d,\ a+3\,d,\ a+4\,d, \ldots$$

The coefficient of d in the second term being one, is one less than the number of the term, and since the coefficient of d increases by unity in the successive terms, it follows that this coefficient will always be less by unity than the number of the term; hence,

$$\text{The } n^{th} \text{ term} = a + (n - 1)d.$$

Take the series, 3, 5, 7, 9, . . .

Then, the 100th term $= 3 + 99 \times 2 = 201$.

The same formula will apply to an infinity of other cases, not one of which was taken into account in establishing the formula. Where is even the shadow of the *petitio principii* in this? The syllogism is liable to this charge only when the major premise is obtained by *real induction*, and then only apparently.

3*d*. *Reasoning in a circle*. This fallacy consists in assuming a premise involving the conclusion, and then from the conclusion deducing the premise. It is analogous to the *petitio principii*. An argument in which the premises involve the conclusion is not to be taken as a case of *petitio principii*, or *reasoning in a circle*, provided the premises be established by evidence independent of the conclusion.

4*th*. *Saltus—leap in logic*. This fallacy consists in suppressing one premise and inferring the conclusion from another with which it has no logical connection, on the assumption that the suppressed premise would justify the conclusion.

5*th*. *Fallacy of Division and Composition*. The fallacy of division occurs when the middle term is used collectively in the major premise, distributively in the minor.

The Greeks overthrew Troy.
Socrates was a Greek.
∴ Socrates overthrew Troy.

The fallacy of composition occurs when the middle term is used distributively in the major premise, and collectively in the minor.

Three and four are two numbers.
Seven is three and four.
∴ Seven is two numbers.

6*th. The fallacy that objects are incompatible because our conceptions of them are incompatible.* M. Comte, the founder of the Positive Philosophy, says: "I must remark upon one very striking truth which becomes apparent during the pursuit of astronomical science—its distinct and ever-increasing opposition, as it attains a higher perfection, to the theological and metaphysical spirit. Theological philosophy supposes every thing to be governed by will, and that phenomena are, therefore, eminently variable, at least virtually. The positive philosophy, on the contrary, conceives them as subject to invariable laws, which permit us to predict with absolute precision.

"The radical incompatibility of these two views is nowhere more marked than in regard to the phenomena of the heavens, since, in that direction, our prevision is proved to be perfect. The punctual arrival of comets and eclipses, with all their train of minute incidents, exactly foretold, long before, by the aid of ascertained laws, must lead the common mind to feel that such events must be free from the control of any will, which could not be will, if it was thus subordinated to our astronomical decisions."

Let us see if the power of prevision is so fatal to theological conceptions as M. Comte would have us believe.

He assumes that a will is necessarily variable and capricious, as is the case to a greater or less extent with respect to the will of man. The phenomena of the heavens are certainly subversive of the idea that the universe is governed by such a will. But it is a theological conception that with God "is no variableness, neither shadow of turning." How is the uniformity of the astronomical laws incompatible with the idea of a God who is "the same yesterday, to-day, and forever?"

It is a theological conception that God created the material universe as the theater on which should act his intelligent creatures. Now, the stability of the material universe, consequent upon the uniformity of the laws of nature, is essential to the continued existence of the inhabitants of the world as they are at present constituted. Hence, since God wills the existence of man on earth, he also wills the uniformity of the laws of nature, and this uniformity, which is an indispensable condition of the act of prevision, is not subversive of theological conceptions, nor incompatible with the idea of a God.

Comte makes one qualification which destroys the supposed incompatibility between astronomical and theological science. He says that theological philosophy, which represents every thing as governed by will, makes phenomena variable, "at least virtually;" but this is perfectly consistent with the fact that *actually*, at least for an indefinite period, phenomena may be *invariable.*

But this uniformity, though observed through a

long period, does not prove that things will always remain as they are at present constituted.

The invariable uniformity of astronomical phenomena, through the period of human history, is perfectly compatible with the sublime declaration, "Of old hast thou laid the foundations of the earth, and the heavens are the work of thy hands. They shall perish, but thou shalt endure: yea, all of them shall wax old like a garment; as a vesture shalt thou change them, and they shall be changed. But thou art the same, and thy years shall have no end."

The unchangeableness of God consists in his purposes which never vary, and is perfectly consistent with the fact that he carries out his plans, in a progressive series of acts to their final consummation.

Again, in reference to Physics, M. Comte says: "With this science begins the exhibition of human power in modifying phenomena. In astronomy, human intervention was out of the question—in physics, it begins; and we shall see how it becomes more powerful as we descend the scale.

"This power counterbalances that of exact prevision which we have in astronomy. The one power or the other—the power of foreseeing or of modifying—is necessary to our outgrowth of theological philosophy. Our prevision disproves the notion that phenomena proceed from a supernatural will, which is the same thing as calling them variable; and our ability to modify them shows that the powers under which they proceed are subordinate to our own. . . .

"As the phenomena of any science become more complex, the first power [that of prevision] decreases, and the other [that of modifying] increases, so that the one or the other is always present to show unquestionably, that the events of the world are not ruled by supernatural will, but by natural laws."

But how does man's power of modifying the circumstances which surround him disprove the fact of a supernatural will? It is God's will that man "should have dominion over the fish of the sea, and over the fowl of the air, and over the cattle, and over all the earth, and over every creeping thing that creepeth upon the earth." This certainly gives man ample license to modify the circumstances which surround him, and cause them to subserve his interests and promote his happiness, and this modification is not subversive of theological conceptions nor incompatible with the idea of a God.

It will be observed that we have not assumed the superfluous task of proving the validity of theological conceptions or the truth of the being of a God, but have shown that Comte has failed to prove the incompatibility of positive philosophy with theological science.

3. Aberrancies.

1. *Definition.*

An aberrancy is a wandering from the conclusion warranted by the premises and drawing another unwarranted.

2. *Classes.*

1*st. Inferring the conclusion false because the premises are false or the reasoning illogical.* In such cases the proper inference is not that the conclusion is false, but that it is not proved.

Suppose a student should fail in his attempt to demonstrate the proposition that, *The square of the hypothenuse of a right-angled triangle is equal to the sum of the squares of the other sides*, would his failure invalidate the proposition?

Aberrancies of this kind are not unfrequent, and are even committed by experienced debaters. Thus, Dr. Rice, in his debate with Mr. Pingree, says: "I have undertaken to prove the conclusion false, by showing the premises on which it is based to be unsound. Is this not a fair mode of reasoning? If the premises are false, the conclusion can not be true. . . . If the principle be false, the conclusion based upon it is certainly false." Dr. Rice should have said, Mr. Pingree has failed to prove his proposition. The conclusion may be objectively true, though one or both of the premises be false, as is seen in the following case:

Every month has thirty days.
April is a month.
∴ April has thirty days.

2*d*. *Inferring the reasoning valid because the conclusion is true.*

It does not follow, because the conclusion is true, that the argument is valid. Many an unsound argument has escaped detection, because the conclusion of the speaker coincided with the opinions of the hearers.

3*d*. *Ambiguity in the conclusion.* This occurs when the conclusion is susceptible of two interpretations, one of which is a legitimate deduction from the premises and the other not. The conclusion is regularly drawn and all seems fair; but the reasoner intentionally or unconsciously passes to the second interpretation, and claims that as the legitimate conclusion.

Thus, in the following example:

Whatever is foreknown must be as foreknown.
Human volitions are foreknown.
∴ Human volitions must be as foreknown.

But this may mean, simply, that it must be true, as a matter of fact, that human volitions are as they are foreknown; or that human volitions are necessitated to be just as they are—that they can not, by any possibility, be otherwise.

Whatever A knows must be as he knows.
A knows that B is present.
∴ B must be present.

A thing must be as known, because it must be known as it is, so far as it is known at all. The assumption of the fact corresponding to the knowledge is a logical necessity to account for the knowledge; but implies nothing in regard to necessity in the thing itself. The fact might have been different, then the knowledge would also have been different.

4*th*. *The fallacy of objections*. This consists in rejecting, as false, that which is liable to objection. The atheistic argument drawn from the fact of moral evil can be thus stated:

If God had been both willing and able to prevent sin, it would not have occurred; but sin has occurred; ∴ God is either able and not willing to prevent it, which is inconsistent with his holiness; or willing and not able, which is inconsistent with his omnipotence; or neither willing nor able, which is inconsistent both with his holiness and his omnipotence; but either of these consequences is destructive of the idea of a God; ∴ there can be no God.

In reply it may be said that God, if he had seen fit, might have created a universe in which all moral evil should be excluded forever. But from such a universe, though displaying infinite perfection in its mechanism, all moral excellence would also be excluded; for, since necessitated action possesses no moral character, moral excellence implies liberty, and liberty involves the possibility of moral evil. Hence, to the mind of God, three alternatives were presented: No universe at all, or a mechanical universe in which all disorder and all moral excellence should be excluded, or a moral universe in which both moral evil and moral excellence should be possible. Who can affirm that the latter alternative was not preferable? Because the omniscient God chose to create a moral universe, shall short-sighted human reason deny his holiness or his omnipotence?

4. Examples of Fallacies.

Let the student point out the fallacies in the following examples:

1. All good fathers provide food and clothing for their children.
   Mr. B. provides food and clothing for his children.
   ∴ Mr. B. is a good father.

2. All moral beings are accountable.
   No brute is a moral being.
   ∴ No brute is accountable.

3. Those who found universities are patrons of learning.
King Alfred founded the University of Oxford.
∴ King Alfred was a great scholar.

4. No pagan is a Christian.
Every villager is a pagan.
∴ No villager is a Christian.

5. No cat has nine tails.
Every cat has one tail more than no cat.
∴ Every cat has ten tails.

6. That side of the river is one side of the river.
This side of the river is not that side of the river.
∴ This side of the river is the other side of the river.

7. If Christianity were from God, it would be universal.
It is not universal.
∴ It is not from God.

8. The fact of knowledge implies a correspondence of nature between the knowing subject and the known object.
Matter is to mind an object of knowledge.
∴ Mind is resolvable into matter, or matter into mind.

9. Things totally unlike can not act upon each other.
Mind and matter are totally unlike.
∴ Mind can not act upon matter.

10. Mind can not act upon matter.
The movements of the body correspond to the relations of the mind.
∴ There is a preëstablished harmony between mind and matter.

11. The volitions of the mind can not cause the movements of the body.
The hypothesis of a preëstablished harmony is untenable.
∴ God causes the movements of the body to correspond with the volitions of the mind.

12. Euathlus, a young man, agreed to pay Protagoras, the prince of sophists, a large sum of money to accomplish him as a legal rhetorician. One half the sum was paid down, and it was agreed that the other half should be paid on the day when Euathlus should plead and gain his first case. But as the scholar was not in so much of a hurry to commence his legal practice as the master to obtain the other half of his fee, Protagoras brought Euathlus into court, and addressed him thus: "Learn, most foolish of young men, that, whether the judges decide in your favor or against you, pay me my demand you must. For if the judgment be against you, I shall obtain the fee by decree of the court, but if in your favor, I shall obtain it by the terms of the contract, since it be comes due on the very day you gain your first case."

To this Euathlus rejoined: "Learn, most sapient of masters, from your own argument, that whatever may be the finding of the court, absolved I must be from any claim by you. For if the decision be favorable, I pay nothing by the sentence of the judges, but if unfavorable, I pay nothing in virtue of the compact, since, though pleading, I shall not have gained my case."

13. "It is an observation which all the world can verify, that there is nothing so deplorable as the conduct of some celebrated mathematicians in their own affairs, nor any thing so absurd as their opinions on the sciences not within their jurisdiction."

Hence, the study of mathematics destroys common sense.

14. There are in all of the professions, even distinguished men, who hold the most absurd opinions on sciences not within their jurisdiction.

Hence, the practice of any profession destroys common sense.

ANALYSIS OF CONTENTS.

www.ingramcontent.com/pod-product-compliance
Lightning Source LLC
LaVergne TN
LVHW021400110826
845150LV00007B/1721

* 9 7 8 1 4 2 5 5 1 3 5 5 9 *